GREAT SPORTING MEMORIES

Compiled by **Keith McCartney**
and **David Corstorphine**

First published 2003 by Geddes & Grosset, David Dale House, New Lanark, ML11 9DJ, Scotland, for the Scottish Motor Neurone Disease Association, 76 Firhill Road, Glasgow, www.scotmnd.org.uk

Compiled by Keith McCartney and David Corstorphine
Designed and edited by Geddes & Grosset

With grateful thanks to all the individual contributors, to the sports desks, picture desks and rights and information departments of The Evening Times, The Herald and the Scottish Daily Record, Colin McPherson and to PA Photo who all provided their services and photographs for free

ISBN 1 84205 300 0

Printed and bound in the UK

FOREWORD
Norrie McArthur

Since I was diagnosed with Motor Neurone Disease (MND) in March 1996, the staff at Waid Academy and friends have participated in annual fundraising events to support the work of the Scottish Motor Neurone Disease Association (SMNDA).

MND is a terminal illness which causes muscle wasting and a deterioration in motor skills. Previous sufferers have included David Niven and Don Revie. There is currently no cure, and in order to assist research by the SMNDA and neurologists, fundraising is essential since currently only £15,000 of government money is received annually by the Association.

Our fundraising events have covered cycling, walking, climbing and, in June 2001, ten of us took part in a parachute jump. The driving force behind the vast majority of these sponsored events has been my colleague Keith McCartney who came up with the idea of compiling this book. Initially he wrote to football managers and people in politics and this produced an excellent response. However, another member of staff, David Corstorphine, and a former pupil of mine, Adam Reid who lives in Rio de Janeiro, also got involved and made many other contacts.

I would like to take this opportunity to thank everyone who contributed to the production of this book and I hope that those who buy it enjoy reading it.

A jubilant Tony Stanger at Murrayfield, 1990 © Scottish Daily Record

ACKNOWLEDGEMENTS
Davie Corstorphine

What's your best sporting memory?

Most people will, when asked this question, allow their eyes to glaze over as they look back on some experience they either witnessed or in which they participated. For me, it could have been Tony Stanger's try against the Auld Enemy at Murrayfield in 1990, when Scotland went on to win the Grand Slam. Or was it jumping up and down in delight as my young son won his heat in the under 10s back crawl at Dundee Swimming Pool? Or perhaps my arms aching, when winching in the jib sheets on board my friend's yacht, as we sailed past Fingal's Cave on Staffa in a Force 4 with wall-to-wall sunshine?

The answer to the question will be different for each of us. Famous people are no exception, and for this book, celebrities the world over have willingly written down what, for them, was that "golden moment".

We all know somebody who knows somebody who is famous. We just need to ask around! That's how the information for this book was gathered – by simply asking others. What's more, these people care enough to contribute to such a worthy cause.

Our thanks go out to all who have assisted with this project, especially Jane Partington at The Waid, Adam Reid in Brazil, Angus Dixon at the BBC, Emil Pacholek at DC Thomson and Craig Stockton of the Scottish Motor Neurone Disease Association.

ACKNOWLEDGEMENTS
Keith McCartney

Whenever sports-minded folk gather the talk invariably turns to memorable moments from the days that have gaen awa. For me nothing can beat the experiences of being at Hampden Park on that magic night in 1973 when Scotland beat Czechoslovakia to qualify for the 1974 World Cup finals and at Ibrox Park on the day Kilmarnock won the Scottish Cup in 1997.

It has been a pleasure and a delight to read the sporting memories contributed by so many people from different walks of life as they have arrived by post and e-mail for this book and I have no doubt you will find equal enjoyment in reading their reminiscences. To all who have given us the privilege of sharing their trip down memory lane, sincere thanks.

The production of this book would not have been possible without the help and support of a great many people. To them we extend our gratitude and would wish to record our special thanks to Ron Grosset, of Geddes & Grosset our publishers, for the sterling work he has done on this publication. Thanks also are due to Ian Watson of SMG, Stuart Nicol and Allan Thompson of The Daily Record for taking the time from their very busy schedules to do picture research and provide photographs for this book.

We hope you enjoy the book!

THE MAN WHO INSPIRED THIS BOOK

Norris McArthur has been involved in sport all of his life. His skills as a footballer saw him play for Lugar Boswell Thistle in the Ayrshire League, Lochore Welfare, Thornton Hibs and St Andrews United in the Fife League, Clachnacuddin, Ross County and Elgin City in the Highland League and Berwick Rangers in the Scottish League. He also had successful spells as manager of Fife Junior clubs St Andrews United and Newburgh.

Away from football, Norrie has played both cricket and rugby for Waid Academy FPs, is a long standing member of Crail Golfing Society and has been a keen participant in raft races.

Norrie was appointed Principal Teacher of Physical Education at Waid Academy in January 1974 from an APT post at Inverness High School and took up his present post as Head of Community Use at the East Neuk School in August 1979.

MY EXPERIENCE WITH ALS (AMYOTRAPHIC LATERAL SCLEROSIS OR MOTOR NEURONE DISEASE)
Professor Stephen W Hawking

I am quite often asked: How do you feel about having ALS? The answer is, not a lot. I try to lead as normal a life as possible, and not think about my condition, or regret the things it prevents me from doing, which are not that many.

It was a great shock to me to discover that I had motor neurone disease. I had never been very well co-ordinated physically as a child. I was not good at ball games, and my handwriting was the despair of my teachers. Maybe for this reason, I didn't care much for sport or physical activities. But things seemed to change when I went to Oxford, at the age of 17. I took up coxing and rowing. I was not Boat Race standard, but I got by at the level of inter-College competition. In my third year at Oxford, however, I noticed that I seemed to be getting clumsier, and I fell over once or twice for no apparent reason.

But it was not until I was at Cambridge, in the following year, that my father noticed, and took me to the family doctor. He referred me to a specialist, and shortly after my 21st birthday, I went into hospital for tests. I was in for two weeks, during which I had a wide variety of tests.

They didn't tell me what I had, except that it was not multiple sclerosis, and that I was an a-typical case. I gathered however, that they expected it to continue to get worse, and that there was nothing they could do, except give me vitamins. I could see that they didn't expect them to have much effect. I didn't feel like asking for more details, because they were obviously bad. The realisation that I had an incurable disease, that was likely to kill me in a few years, was a bit of a shock. How could something like that happen to me? Why should I be cut off like this? However, while I had been in hospital, I had seen a boy I vaguely knew die of leukemia, in the bed opposite me. It had not been a pretty sight. Clearly there were people who were worse off than me. At least my condition didn't make me feel sick. Whenever I feel inclined to feel sorry for myself I remember that boy.

The doctors told me to go back to Cambridge and carry on with the research I had just started in general relativity and cosmology. But I was not making much progress, because I didn't have much mathematical background. And anyway, I might not live long enough to finish my PhD.

Before my condition had been diagnosed, I had been very bored with life. There had not seemed to be anything worth doing. But shortly after I came out of hospital, I dreamt I was going to be executed. I suddenly realised that there were a lot of worthwhile things I could do if I were reprieved. Another dream that I had several times was that I would sacrifice my life to save others. After all, if I was going to die anyway, it might as well do some good. But I didn't die. In fact, although there was a cloud hanging over my future, I found to my surprise, that I was enjoying life in the present more than before. I began to make progress with my research, and I got engaged to a girl called Jane Wilde, who I had met just about the time my condition was diagnosed. That engagement changed my life. It gave me something to live for. But it also meant that I had to get a job if we were to get married. I therefore applied for a research fellowship at Gonville and Caius (pronounced Keys) College, Cambridge.

To my great surprise, I got a fellowship, and we got married a few months later. The fellowship at Caius took care of my immediate employment problem. I was lucky to have chosen to work in theoretical physics, because that was one of the few areas in which my condition would not be a serious handicap. And I was fortunate that my scientific reputation increased, at the same time that my disability got worse. This meant that people were prepared to offer me a sequence of positions in which I only had to do research, without having to lecture.

Up until 1974, I was able to feed myself, and get in and out of bed. Jane managed to help me, and bring up our three children, without outside help. However, things were getting more difficult, so we took to having one of my research students living with us. In return for free accommodation, and a lot of my attention, they helped me get up and go to bed. In 1980, we changed to a system of community and private nurses. This lasted until I caught pneumonia in 1985. I had to have a tracheostomy operation. After this, I had to have 24-hour nursing care.

Before the operation, my speech had been getting more

slurred, so that only a few people who knew me well, could understand me. But at least I could communicate. I wrote scientific papers by dictating to a secretary, and I gave seminars through an interpreter, who repeated my words more clearly. However, the tracheostomy operation removed my ability to speak altogether.

For a time, the only way I could communicate was to spell out words letter by letter, by raising my eyebrows when someone pointed to the right letter on a spelling card. However, a computer expert in California, called Walt Woltosz sent me a computer program he had written, called Equaliser. This allowed me to select words from a series of menus on the screen, by pressing a switch in my hand. A switch, operated by head or eye movement, could also control the program. When I have built up what I want to say, I can send it to a speech synthesiser. This system allowed me to communicate much better than I could before. I can manage up to 15 words a minute.

Using this system, I have written a book, and dozens of scientific papers. I have also given many scientific and popular talks. They have all been well received.

I have had motor neurone disease for practically all my adult life. Yet it has not prevented me from having a very attractive family, and being successful in my work. This is thanks to the help I have received from Jane, my children, and a large number of other people and organisations. I have been lucky, that my condition has progressed more slowly than often is the case. But it shows that one need not lose hope.

PAUL ACKFORD
Rugby union writer and former British Lions forward

My favourite sporting moment was winning the third test with the Lions in Australia in 1989. The decisive moment came when David Campese tried to run out from behind the Australian's posts; he passed to his full-back, who wasn't expecting the ball, and when it flopped on the ground Ieuan Evans dived on it.

That try was the turning point and we went on to clinch the series. I remember it all so clearly – I was watching from 60 metres away!

KATE ADIE
BBC News Correspondent

I was once a sports reporter in local radio – for about an afternoon.

Sadly, not for me the glories of Manchester United. Even so, I set off with great enthusiasm for Evenwood Town's ground – an interesting patch of sloping moorland in the higher reaches of County Durham.

It was a grey afternoon, with just a hint of drizzle, and the crowd on the sidelines matched the teams – twenty or so each. As play swung from one end of the pitch to the other, the keen knot of supporters trekked this way and that for a better view, for a heavy fog was descending.

My radio car was anchored behind one goal, and I grew increasingly bothered as most of the action took place in the distant half. Shouts occasionally drifted out of the mist, some sounding suspiciously like celebration, some sounding like roars of frustration. There was no-one within hailing distance, as I heard the sports programme's half-time round-up being announced on my headphones.

I decided to be honest, and delivered thus:

"Evenwood Town one, Crook Town two, possibly three, or maybe the other way round."

Somehow, I never became a permanent member of the sports reporting team.

PATRICK BARCLAY
Football correspondent for *The Sunday Telegraph*

My favourite sporting memory is Dundee winning the Scottish League championship in 1962, closely followed by the start of the European Cup campaign the following season. We were drawn against Cologne, who were among the favourites, and the fans went in some awe, hoping our heroes could get away with a draw or even a respectable defeat.

We won 8–1. It was pinch-yourself time. In the end, we lost in the semi-finals having also knocked out Sporting Lisbon and Anderlecht. Imagine the fuss if Rangers or Celtic did that now!

DAVE BASSETT
Manager, Leicester City Football Club

My most memorable moment is of the 1966 World Cup final where England beat West Germany 4–2 after extra-time at Wembley.

Our ref: DTB/CMc/C3947

28 March 2002

Mr K McCartney
Waid Academy

Dear Mr McCartney

Thank you for your letter dated 7 March enquiring as to my most memorable sporting occasion for inclusion in a booklet which you are producing to raise funds for the Scottish Motor Neurone Disease Association.

My most memorable moment is of the 1966 World Cup Final where England beat West Germany 4-2 after extra-time at Wembley.

Good luck with your fundraising efforts.

Yours sincerely

DAVE BASSETT
Manager

LEICESTER CITY FOOTBALL CLUB PLC
TRAINING GROUND, MIDDLESEX ROAD, AYLESTONE, LEICESTER LE2 8PB. TEL: (0116) 291 5279 FAX: (0116) 291 5278
WEBSITE ADDRESS: www.lcfc.com

JOHN BEATTIE
Scotland and British Lions rugby player and commentator

My favourite sporting memory as a spectator is of being on a French campsite with my young family as France won the 1998 world cup. Players like Zidane were magical, and the whole of France was taken over by the sheer exuberance of that match and the beauty of it too.

The best moment of my own sporting career was beating England by 33–6, the record score, in 1986, when we had been told they were unbeatable. We were very fit, having trained most days with the national squad.

I was to hit their second-row Maurice Colclough early in the game to unsettle him. Everyone except me thought it was a really good idea. We also had extra balls on the touch line to speed the game up. Despite my nerves, the night before the game I slept like a baby – I wet my bed three times.

We went down to the pitch on Saturday with everybody reminding me to hit Maurice Colclough, and I was so excited upon kick-off that I ran into a bloke called Wade Dooley instead. The ref threatened to send me off. "But I've still to hit Maurice Colclough!" I said in my desperation!

Anyway, there were great tries by Matt Duncan, John Rutherford and Scott Hastings, and it was hugely enjoyable to be part of a great team with the likes of Finlay Calder, Scott and Gavin Hastings, and the likes of Roy Laidlaw, Colin Deans, and Ian Paxton in the side too.

TONY BLAIR
Prime Minister

The Prime Minister feels it is very important to keep fit in his job and his two great loves are tennis and football which he tries to play as often as he can.

From the Private Secretary

10 DOWNING STREET
LONDON SW1A 2AA

Dear Mr McCartney

I am writing on behalf of the Prime Minister to thank you for your le 7 March requesting that he write to you describing his most memorable spo occasion which could then be included in a booklet you are producing to raise funds for the Scottish Motor Neurone Disease Association.

I am afraid there are far too many occasions for the Prime Minister to be able to single out any one sporting moment. However, he does try and make time for sport. Indeed, he feels it is very important to keep fit in his job and his two great loves are tennis and football which he tries to play as often as he can.

With best wishes,

Yours sincerely

KATIE KAY

Prime Minister Tony Blair

© Scottish Daily Record

ALAN BLEASDALE
Playwright and author

I was nine years old and wanted to play for the under-11s' football team. I thought they were crap and kept pestering the teacher, telling him I was good enough. Eventually he picked me, telling me I was in at left-back. I didn't know where left-back was on the field, so I ran home and got my dad out of bed – he was working nights – and asked him. He drew me a diagram.

At 4pm that day, he was on the sidelines when I ran out. We got beat 4–0, but I did head a corner off the line. That's all I can remember. From then on, my dad was there every time I played.

SIR MICHAEL BONALLACK
Golfer

Without doubt my most memorable sporting occasion was the 1971 Walker Cup Match on the Old Course at St Andrews when I was playing-captain of the team representing Great Britain and Ireland.

Up until then, Great Britain had only previously won the Cup on one occasion and that was at St Andrews in 1938. So, as you can imagine, the pressure on the team to try and regain the trophy after a gap of 33 years was intense and in fact some members of the press had already some three weeks prior to the match written off our chances, on the basis that some of our players were too young and too inexperienced. The golf correspondent for *The Financial Times* went so far as to say that if we won he would gladly jump fully clothed into the Swilcan Burn.

On the first day of the match we got off to a great start winning all four foursomes in the morning however, as they are apt to do, the Americans came storming back in the afternoon winning 6 $1/2$ of the singles to our 1 $1/2$ leaving us trailing by one point at the half way stage. The next morning we only managed 1 $1/2$ points from the four foursomes, which meant we had to win 5 $1/2$ points from the afternoon singles to capture the Cup. At this stage many spectators decided they would leave, not imagining they would miss a unique occasion.

I myself played top against Lanny Wadkins who beat me on the 17th green and so quickly did we play that, when we finished, the next match was still only half-way down the 14th fairway.

There was a large scoreboard at the 17th green, in front of which I sat and it showed that nearly all the matches were extremely close except in the last where Tom Kite had established a 3-hole lead against Geoffrey Marks.

In the past, when matches have been as close as this at the end, the Americans, with their great experience, seemed to play better but this time the reverse happened and match after match showed the GB & I team edging ahead. Hugh Stewart beat Vinny Giles and Warren Humphrey beat Steve Melnyk and then a roar went up on the 18th Green when Charlie Green beat Allan Miller by one hole. I was still at the 17th green when Roddy Carr holed an enormous putt across the 18th to beat Jim Symons, followed by George McGregor and Jimmy Gabrielsen also victorious on the same green. This meant we only needed one half point to win and at that very moment David Marsh, who was one-up on Bill Hyman, hit a magnificent second shot with a three-iron, into the 17th green to finish some eight feet from the flag. Although Hyman managed to half the hole it meant that the half point was secured and the Walker Cup was back in Britain.

The celebrations that night went on almost until dawn and although a number of people fell into the Swilcan Burn *The Financial Times* correspondent was not one of them. The caddies went looking for him at the entrance to the press tent, to make sure he kept his promise, but he managed to cut his way out of the back of the tent and was last seen running as fast as he could to his car parked in West Sands.

This will always remain my most memorable sporting event.

JENNIE BOND
BBC Royal Correspondent

When I was about eleven, a flame-haired Irish hockey teacher selected me for the school hockey team. I played right wing and one of my duties in that role was to roll in the ball in a strategic manner. It had to be rolled along the ground, but I got so wound up about it that I forgot to let go of the ball and threw it up into the air. It was lobbed across the whole pitch, everyone laughed, the game was stopped and I never played hockey again!

ANDY BOWMAN
Former player, Heart of Midlothian and Chelsea Football Clubs

One of my most memorable moments in my football career was whilst playing with Heart of Midlothian.

We won the Scottish League Championship in season 1957/58 and in the process we set a new record for the top division – 132 goals in 34 games.

EDITH BOWMAN
Television presenter and Waid Academy former pupil

I was always pretty average at sport at school although I did like to have a go. I remember hockey on freezing Saturday mornings on the bus to play Auchmuty, house matches playing netball and I remember winning the shot-put at one particular sports day.

Last year I had one of the most memorable experiences ever, never mind sporting. It was the last ever game to be played at Wembley before they closed it and a charity match had been arranged between a Scotland select versus an England select.

I got to the changing rooms where we were given our strips: Bowman number 7. It doesn't get much better I thought. So, we are all lined up in the tunnel: Rod Stewart, Justin Currie, Andy Gray (just a few of those in Scotland shirts), Cat Deeley, Audley Harrison, Atomic Kitten, David Platt (a few of those in the Auld Enemy shirts). Suddenly the Scots started singing "Flower of Scotland" as we left the tunnel and headed round the track to the pitch.

The stadium wasn't exactly capacity, in fact I think there were only about 300 people there, but it didn't matter. They played crowd noises over the PA system and the hairs on my arms stood to attention. I think I even had a tear in my eye, and the great thing was that I managed to convince the organisers to let my wee brother play. So there we were, the two of us, playing for Scotland at Wembley. Rod Stewart even passed me the ball up the wing. And, to top it all off, we won thanks to a late-minute winner from Mark Ferguson, son of Sir Alex. As you can expect the celebrations went on into the wee small hours. Definitely a money-can't-buy experience that I will never, ever forget!

Edith Bowman   © Scottish Daily Record

CRAIG BROWN

Former Scotland Manager. Manager of Preston North End, Football Club.

A favourite sporting memory of mine is being the only coach ever to have guided Scotland to a World Cup final. It was with the under-17s in 1989 and what made it extra-special was that the tournament was held in Scotland. After beating Portugal – Figo and all – in the semi-finals in front of a full house at Tynecastle we took on Saudi

Craig Brown with former first minister Henry McLeish
© Scottish Daily Record/Craig Halkett

Arabia at Hampden Park, where 53,000 saw us lose only on penalties.

We subsequently had some great moments with the seniors in World Cups and European Championship – but nothing beat getting to that final with the youths.

GORDON BROWN
Chancellor of the Exchequer

My passion for football started a long time before I ever got to see the national team play. I grew up in Fife, part of which I now represent at Westminster. My earliest football memories are of Stark's Park, the Kirkcaldy home of Raith Rovers. Indeed, my introduction to market forces was a season spent attempting to sell programmes outside the ground.

It was my father – a Church of Scotland minister but a keen follower of our national game – who first took me along to football matches, and together we travelled around Fife, seeing the local teams play. All my schooldays I turned to the sports pages long before I turned to news or politics.

Those 1960s games were my first exposure to Cowdenbeath's unique style. The team is much loved and it's home record in the 1993–94 season – a long run of bad luck when it failed to win at Central Park until it beat Arbroath 1–0 on 2nd April – made it famous throughout Britain.

Such reputations are by definition temporary; in the Scottish League, life goes on. A new season puts one firmly in the past: who knows what glories now await the "Blue Brazils" of Cowdenbeath? Their ground is better than ever – cruel local humour about an all-seated stadium and a three-piece suite notwithstanding. As the local MP, I was delighted to receive an invitation to the official opening of the ground improvements, so can now con-clusively deny this calumny.

I have followed Scotland's World Cup ambitions ever since I was a schoolboy. I was one of thousands of teenagers who stayed off school when Scotland had to beat Italy to qualify for the 1966 finals in England – and failed to do so. As schoolboys, we were serious about

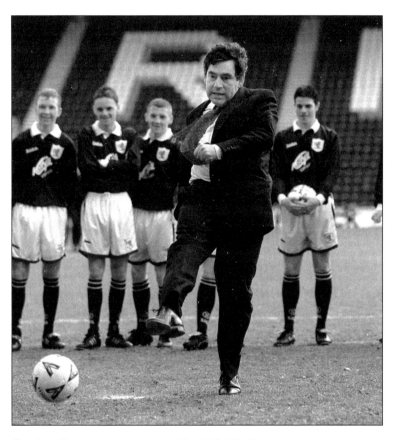

Gordon Brown scores a penalty at Raith Rovers
© Gordon Jack/Scottish Daily Record

Scotland. According to local legend, the headmaster in the adjoining school belted the boys in the morning for playing truant in the afternoon. He punished them in advance because he knew that he could rely upon them – to support Scotland.

You start young and you can't give up supporting Scotland. You can't walk out simply because they're playing badly. You'll be there, irrespective of standards, performance, bad luck and the usual – mainly defensive and goalkeeping – errors that come from nowhere to snatch defeat from the jaws of victory for Scotland yet again. Once disappointed before, twice we turn up, and as optimists. Scotland's like that.

Yet the fanaticism that has characterised Scotland's following – of which I can claim to be a part for many years – of the national football team still demands some explanation. You need only to recall the scenes of delirium among the Scottish football fans when the team beat England 3–2 at Wembley in 1967 – when they tore up bits of turf to take home as a living memento – to realise that clearly there was a lot more at stake than the result of 22 men kicking a ball around. 1967 was surely one of the greatest hours for the boys in blue. I was 16 then, but I still remember the humbling of England – on the very pitch on which they had been crowned only a year previously as champions of the world – by the skills and audacity of "Slim Jim" Baxter, one of my heroes. It was both a Home International and a European Championship qualifier. In Scotland, that day is still thought of as the real World Cup decider. I feel similarly about the 2–1 win at Hampden, in 1976, when Dalglish slid the winner through the legs of a disbelieving Clemence.

Wee boys still have kick-abouts in the street, dreaming of glory. Old men in pubs will tell you what they have seen and what might have been. Middle-aged men like myself watch and hope.

Who knows? .... Some day ... And, if worst comes to worst, we still beat England sometimes.

GEORGE BURLEY
Former manager of Ipswich Town Football Club

My most memorable moment in football would have to be when Ipswich Town got into the Premiership via Wembley on May 29th 2000.

We had been so close for three years, and so to get to Wembley and win was tremendous. I think it was my biggest achievement and from a fan's point of view I'm glad we did it via Wembley.

George Burley celebrating the Premiership promotion for Ipswich

© Scottish Daily Record

TOMMY BURNS
Celtic Football Club

My most memorable sporting occasion as a spectator was Celtic vs Dukla Prague in 1967.

Celtic won 3–2 with Billy McNeill scoring with a last minute header to win the game. As a ten-year-old in an 80,000 crowd it was a fantastic experience.

Celtic FC v Dukla Prague, 1967   © Scottish Daily Record

ERIC CALDOW

Former defender and captain of Glasgow Rangers, capped 40 times for Scotland

There have been many memorable occasions for me.

There was the thrill of walking up the marble staircase in 1950 to be signed for Rangers by the greatest domestic manager of all time, Mr Bill Struth; winning my 1st medal and then captaining Rangers; followed by the great honour of playing for my country. I thought that this was the highest award for any player but I was wrong again.

The greatest moment was when I was chosen as the greatest left back Scotland has ever produced, in the team of the Hampden heroes – that was icing on the cake.

Another great honour happened recently when I was honoured in the hall of fame at Ibrox.

Eric, captain of Rangers FC, held aloft with cup   © SMG Newspapers Ltd

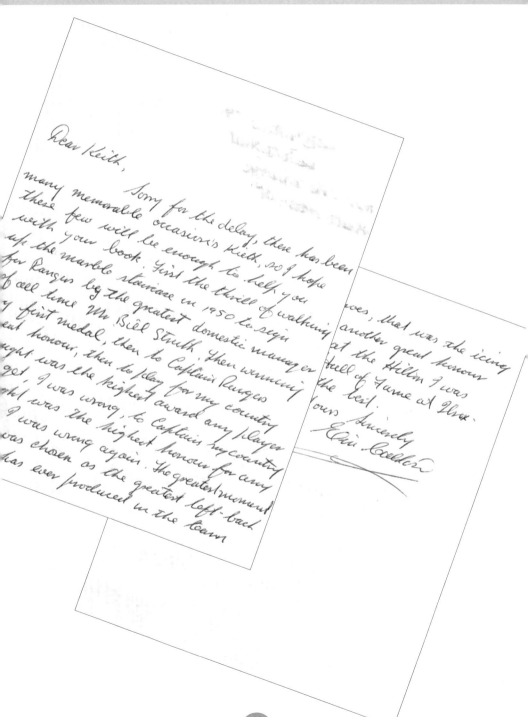

Dear Keith,

Sorry for the delay, there has been many memorable occasion's Keith, so I hope these few will be enough to help you with your book. First the thrill of walking up the marble staircase in 1950 to sign for Rangers by the greatest domestic manager of all time Mr Bill Struth. Then winning my first medal, then to Captain Rangers great honour, then to play for my country that was the highest award any player can get, I was wrong, to Captain my country that was the highest honour for any country I was wrong again. The greatest moment I was chosen as the greatest left-back has ever produced in the team

...es, that was the icing... another great honour... at the Hilton I was... Hull of Fame at Ibrox... the best.

Yours Sincerely

Eric Caldow

ALASTAIR CAMPBELL

Government Director of Communications and Strategy

I have quite a few bad memories of playing rugby at school, because I broke a number of limbs at different times.

My best golfing memory was at Troon, the day after The Open (the year Gene Sarazen got a hole in one on the Postage Stamp). At the end of a dreadful round, I holed out from the fairway on the 18th in front of dozens of workers who were dismantling the stands round the green.

My worst golfing memory was when I made a complete idiot of myself at St Andrews, watched by the world's media, who were covering the Commonwealth Summit. I'd actually been playing OK, but the minute I saw a load of photographers lined up on the 18th, I went to bits, hit two balls out of bounds and another into water. One journalist said the next day it was like watching a cave man swing for his lunch!

Most of my spectating highlights (and desperate moments) have been following Burnley. The best moments include beating Leeds away 4–1 to end their record unbeaten run, beating Spurs away 4–1 in the League Cup when we were in the third division, as well as a number of promotions and relegation survivals. I was also at the Manchester United v Bayern Champions League final in Barcelona, the last few minutes of which were pulsating. I was with my elder son, who (sadly!) is a Manchester United fan. I remember saying to him: "Enjoy this. As sporting excitement goes, it will never get better than this for you."

10 DOWNING STREET
LONDON SW1A 2AA

Director of Communications and Strategy

Dear Keith

13 March 2002

Thank you for your letter of 7 March.

I have quite a few bad memories of playing rugby at school, because I broke a number of limbs at different times. My best golfing memory was at Troon, the day after the British Open (the year Gene Sarazen got a hole in one on the Postage Stamp). At the end of a dreadful round, I holed out from the fairway on the 18th in front of dozens of workers who were dismantling the stands round the green. My worst golfing memory was when I made a complete idiot of myself at St. Andrews, watched by the world's media, who were covering the Commonwealth Summit. I'd actually been playing ok but the minute I saw a load of photographers lined up on the 18th, I went to bits, hit two balls out of bounds, and another into water. One journalist said the next day it was like watching a caveman swing for his lunch.

Most of my spectating highlights (and desperate moments) have been following Burnley. The best moments include beating Leeds away 4-1 to end their record unbeaten run, beating Spurs away 4-1 in the League Cup when we were in the 3rd division, as well as a number of promotions and relegation survivals. I was also at the Manchester United v Bayern Champions league final in Barcelona, the last few minutes of which were pulsating. I was with my elder son, who sadly is a Manchester United fan. I remember saying to him: "Enjoy this. As sporting excitement goes, it will never get better than this for you.".

ALASTAIR CAMPBELL

Keith McCartney
The Waid Academy

MENZIES CAMPBELL

MP for Northeast Fife and Liberal Democrat Spokesperson for Foreign Affairs and Defence

One memory stands out for me above all others. For every athlete, nothing compares with competing in an Olympic Final, even if only in a relay! In 1964, together with Peter Radford, Ron Jones and Lynn Davies, I ran in the four-times 100-metres relay at the Tokyo Olympic Games.

We finished eighth out of eight, but with a new United Kingdom Record. For just less than 40 seconds I had the privilege to compete together with the 31 fastest men in the world. I was scared stiff throughout, but I still remember it as if it was yesterday.

DENNIS CANAVAN
MSP for Falkirk West

It was the day before my 12th birthday. I was on holiday in St Andrews in August 1954 when the Commonwealth (and Empire!) Games were taking place in Vancouver. We had no TV and were very dependent on radio and the press for news of what was happening but the events of that day are still etched in my memory as if I were there.

Roger Bannister had just won gold for England in the mile. The cheering for his victory had hardly died down when Jim Peters of England staggered into the stadium on the last stage of the marathon. He was on his last legs but still well in front with only a lap of the stadium to go. There was a sudden lull in the applause when Peters collapsed. For a full two minutes, he lay still and, although police and medics gathered around him, they knew that physically assisting him would mean disqualification.

Peters managed to rise unsteadily to his feet, tried to carry on but almost immediately his legs gave way. Yet again he struggled to his feet but he reeled from side to side of the track and went down again. Fifteen minutes after he had entered the stadium, he had covered only 150 yards. At last he crossed what he thought was the finishing line and was carried exhausted from the track. He did not realise that he still had 200 yards to go. The line he crossed was the finishing line for the mile event. Jim Peters was down and out.

Shortly afterwards, a little-known Scot called Joe

McGee ran into the stadium. He held off a challenge from two South Africans to win the marathon in 2 hours 39 minutes and 36 seconds. Not the fastest marathon in the world, but surely one of the most dramatic in the history of the event.

McGee never got the credit that he deserved. Like now, many of the sports commentators were biased towards England. Peters was acclaimed as a national hero and there were even demands for the Queen to strike a special medal in his honour.

Joe McGee scarcely rated a mention despite the fact that he won the race. On the day, he judged the hot, humid conditions better than anyone else. He paced himself accordingly and he ran the race to the finish.

It was a gold for Scotland. What a day to remember!

LORD CARRINGTON
Former **NATO** Secretary General and former **UK** Foreign Secretary

Whilst living in Australia in the 1950s I stayed at a remote property in the North West. After dinner my host said to me: "Would you like to shoot a crocodile in our bill-abong?"

So, armed with a shotgun, we embarked in a boat. "If you see two little red eyes, shoot between them, those are the eyes of the crocodile," he said. This I did and whilst the crocodile was being retrieved the boat lurched and my host's torch illuminated a large kangaroo. "Shoot the damn thing!" he cried, "It's an infernal nuisance!" So I did!

I can't think there are many people that had a right and left for a crocodile and a kangaroo.

SANDY CLARK
Former footballer with Rangers, West Ham and Heart of Midlothian, and manager of St Johnstone Football Club

Watching the Brazil 1970 World Cup Team has to be one of my favourite all time memories. However, my favourite moment comes not from my playing career but my management career.

It was leading St Johnstone to third place in the SPL – their highest-ever league placing and also European football. Third place was clinched in a dramatic last day when a Paul Kane goal gave the Saints victory over Dundee by 1–0.

St Johnstone, victorious over Dundee   © Scottish Daily Record

BOB CRAMPSEY
Sports journalist

Real and Eintracht: I would have liked to have been more original but this European Cup final of 1960 so out-topped all other games that I have to stick with it.

It was played on a beautiful spring evening at Hampden. The crowd behaved magnificently, since no Scottish team was involved, and we had gone to see Eintracht who had beaten Rangers 12–4 on aggregate and therefore had to be the best side in the world.

Real Madrid versus Eintracht Frankfurt, 1960   © SMG Newspapers Ltd

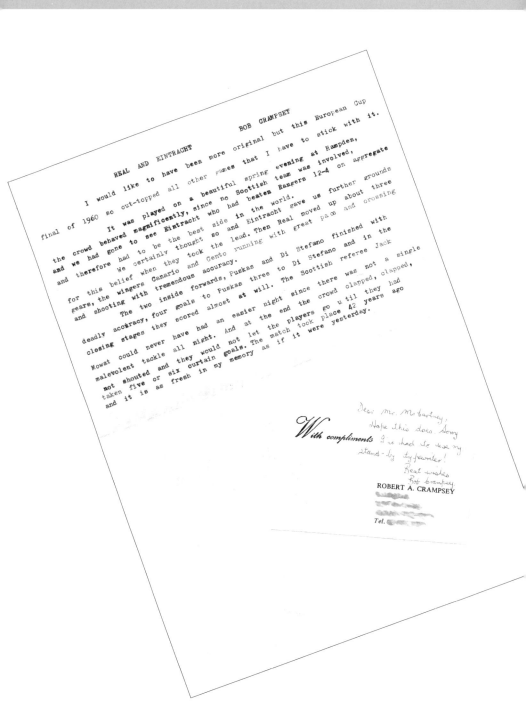

REAL AND EINTRACHT

BOB CRAMPSEY

I would like to have been more original but this European Cup final of 1960 so out-topped all other games that I have to stick with it.

It was played on a beautiful spring evening at Hampden, the crowd behaved magnificently, since no Scottish team was involved, and we had gone to see Eintracht who had beaten Rangers 12-4 on aggregate and therefore had to be the best side in the world.

We certainly thought so and Eintracht gave us further grounds for this belief when they took the lead. Then Real moved up about three gears, the wingers Canario and Gento running with great pace and crossing and shooting with tremendous accuracy.

The two inside forwards, Puskas and Di Stefano finished with deadly accuracy, four goals to Puskas three to Di Stefano and in the closing stages they scored almost at will. The Scottish referee Jack Mowat could never have had an easier night since there was not a single malevolent tackle all night. And at the end the crowd clapped, clapped, not shouted and they would not let the players go until they had taken five or six curtain goals. The match took place 42 years ago and it is as fresh in my memory as if it were yesterday.

With compliments

Dear Mr. McCartney,
Hope this does. Sorry I've had to use my stand-by typewriter!
Best wishes
Bob Crampsey

ROBERT A. CRAMPSEY

Tel.

We certainly thought so, and Eintracht gave us further grounds for this belief when they took the lead. Then Real moved up about three gears, the wingers Canario and Gento running with the great pace and crossing and shooting with tremendous accuracy.

The two inside forwards, Puskas and Di Stephano finished with deadly accuracy, four goals to Puskas, three to Di Stephano and in the closing stages they scored almost at will. The Scottish referee Jack Mowat could never have had an easier night since there was not a single malevolent tackle all night. And at the end the crowd clapped, not shouted, and they would not let the players go until they had taken five or six curtain goals.

The match took place 42 years ago and it is as fresh in my memory as if it were yesterday.

MICHAEL CRICK
BBC TV reporter and author of biographies of Jeffrey Archer and Sir Alex Ferguson

Lancashire v Gloucestershire, Gillette Cup semi-final, 28 July, 1971.

Only once have I ever cheated my way into a sports ground. As a 13-year-old Manchester schoolboy in the summer of 1971, I was so impatient for football to resume that I took up the next best thing – watching Lancashire at one-day cricket. In those days, the other Old Trafford offered a much greater prospect of silverware, as Lancashire were the masters of the limited over game.

They attracted huge crowds. Indeed, on the Wednesday of the Gillette Cup semi-final my friend Hamish and I found ourselves locked out, the victims of a capacity crowd. Unwilling to return home without trying every possibility, we went round the back, scrambled along the railway line and found a hole in the fence just big enough to take our teenage frames.

Inside we joined other boys on the grass behind the rope. And it was there, friends told me later, that I was captured very briefly by live BBC cameras – my first appearance on TV, the medium that eventually became my profession.

Gloucestershire, with the great South African all-rounder Mike Procter, were formidable opponents. They made 229 in their innings, and Lancashire replied slowly before rain stopped play around teatime. The umpires faced a dilemma of whether to disappoint the vast crowd and return the next day. Instead, they famously pressed on, producing one of the latest finishes of all time. Lancashire were still batting as the hands on the town hall clock neared 9pm, and the moon even appeared in the rapidly fading light. With five overs left, Lancashire were still 26 runs short with three wickets remaining, making Gloucestershire favourites.

But then David Hughes strode onto the pitch to bat a number 9 and whacked 4, 6, 2, 2, 6 and another 4 in one over – 24 in all – from the unfortunate John Mortimore, the most celebrated over in the history of one-day county cricket. Two more runs secured Lancashire's trip to Lords where they lifted the cup for the second year running.

One Old Trafford ground has given me numerous moments of excitement, but none in such bizarre circumstances as the July dusk at the cricket ground. Thirty years on, if Lancashire were to bill me for that stolen experience, even making due allowance for inflation, I'd happily cough up. It's such an indelible memory.

ALAN CURBISHLEY
Former footballer with **West Ham and Aston Villa and Manager of Charlton Athletic Football Club**

Charlton Athletic v Sunderland. 1st Division Play Off Final 1998.

This game at Wembley has gone down as one of the top six of the 20th Century and has to be the most memorable for me during my career as a football player/manager.

From the moment we reached the final and the good luck messages started to arrive from supporters all over the world it was something very special.

The day itself was a mixture of every emotion one can feel, from leaving our hotel for the short journey to Wembley, arriving in the dressing room and the feeling that for some players it was going to be the game of their lives. Leading the team out was for me a very proud moment and one I shall always remember. Once the game kicked off the nerves took over, before the joy of going into the lead with the first goal of Clive Mendonca's hat trick. The result was all square at the end of 90 minutes and the thought of another 30 minutes of nervous tension took over. I, like many of the players, was feeling exhausted.

Then came the penalties and that save, which meant we were in The Premiership for the first time in the club's history: my most memorable sporting moment.

Alan Curbishley   © PA Photo/Sean Dempsey

TAM DALYELL
MP for Linlithgow

My favourite sporting memories:

As a spectator: being present with 133,000 others, and 121 pupils of mine from Bo'ness Academy, at the European Cup Final; final result Real Madrid 7, Frankfurt Eintracht 3; being amazed at the skills of Alfredo De Stefano, Ferenc Puskas, El Bicyclo Gento and others at their sparkling best.

Personally: being "last out" when Gary Kasparov took on seven Lords, seven Clerks of the House and seven MPs in a simultaneous chess match versus the British Parliament in 1990.

Real Madrid versus Frankfurt Eintracht, 1960   © SMG Newspapers Ltd

JOCK DAVIDSON
Scotland rugby player

"You have been picked to play in the match Scotland v England at Twickenham [in 1959]. A No. 8 jersey will be provided. Please bring your boots. Blue stockings and white shorts can be obtained from Forsyth's in Princes Street."

Running out onto the pitch at Twickenham in front of an 87,000 crowd, you would think that would be the pinnacle of my sporting career.

No, it's closer to home than that.

1950, the Scottish School's Championships at Anniesland in Glasgow where I was the first Waid Academy pupil to win a Schools' championship medal for the triple jump (in those times it was called the hop step and jump)

The following Monday morning assembly, I was congratulated by Rector Thomson, and the spontaneous applause that erupted after that announcement, the souvenir remains with me to this day. Recognition by one's peers is recognition indeed.

DR KEN DEANS
University of Otago, New Zealand

The All Blacks were playing the June 2000 touring side from Scotland at Carisbrook, Dunedin, "Further Down Under". Suffice to say that despite our constant cheering, shouts of "FREEDOM!" and the dispersing of around 250 "Flower of Scotland" song sheets to everyone around us, we were beaten.

Deciding the lads needed all the encouragement they could get, we took our small posse of Scots and Kiwis to clap them aboard their coach. It was a cold night and some previously consumed beer was beginning to make its presence known.

Finding myself in need of relief I pondered the options: go looking for a toilet and risk missing the team, go behind the bus and risk getting my collar felt (not really an option as A. I am a good law-abiding citizen and B. I was flying out to Argentina the next morning) or use the facilities on the team coach.

The latter appealed and I seized my opportunity when the security man was off his guard. I ran, be-kilted up the bus and made it to the toilet before the burly coach guard made it to the pleats o' ma kilt. I emerged some few minutes later feeling much better but pondering the nature of the reception committee.

To my further relief he was chuckling and wearing a huge grin. As I descended the steps it became obvious that I had in fact boarded the All Blacks' coach. I stopped at the top of the steps for an impromptu photo opportunity. Without hesitation I whipped my harmonica out from my sporran and gave a rousing rendition of Flower of Scotland from the steps. Rapturous applause from the crowd ensued. Considering myself lucky this far I immediately sped off in the direction of the "other" bus lest Mr Lomu be first out of the stadium heading for "his" bus.

We clapped the Scots and retired to the pub for the obligatory post-match post-mortem. I made it to Argentina though my voice took another two days to join me.

BARBARA DICKSON
Singer and actress

The best sporting memory of mine is watching my own children play rugby for their various schools. They have been encouraged and well coached in the game and get enormous pleasure from playing. My eldest son, at school in Yorkshire, played in a sevens tournament last winter and although it was the coldest and wettest day I can recall, the spirit was mighty!

I like the competitive aspect of the game and the introduction of children to the possibility of failure, as well as success. Life is littered with both!

DAVID DIMBLEBY
BBC journalist and broadcaster

I have always hated sport both as a player and a spectator, except sailing. I remember particularly loathing playing in goal at hockey at school and even hid in the lava-
tories to avoid having to go out into the field on an icy
and foggy February day.

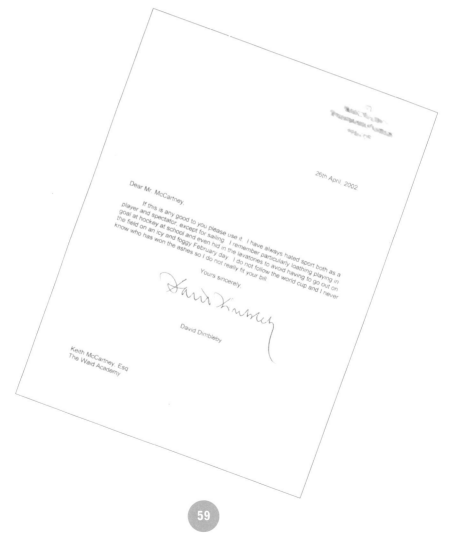

DOUGIE DONNELLY
BBC Scotland sports correspondent

All any sportsman or woman can ask is to be given the chance; to be allowed the responsibility to score the last-minute winning goal or conversion, or hole the four-foot putt to win the tournament.

The great athletes are those who seize the moment – and, as someone fortunate enough to have attended many of the world's great sporting occasions over the last 20 years, I have witnessed many such "moments".

One of the greatest, and certainly most emotional, came early in 2002, at the Winter Olympic Games in Salt Lake City.

The two all-Scottish teams representing Great Britain both arrived in Utah as medal contenders. But while Harry Macmillan's men's team found things going all wrong for them both on and off the ice, it was a different story for Rhona Martin's women's rink.

As confidence grew after a nervous start, qualification for the medal play-offs seemed certain, until a last stone defeat at the hands of the host nation, and then, a seemingly fatal reverse to the Germans, looked to have ended team GB's hopes.

But the Swiss then beat Germany to allow Rhona's team a back door entry into the tie-breakers, and the girls took full advantage.

Victory over the much-fancied Swedes and revenge against Germany set up the Martin team for a semi-final

The Olympic gold medal-winning British women's curling team
© Colin McPherson

with Canada, the world's most powerful curling nation.

Amidst growing excitement in the Ogden Ice Arena, Martin's team pulled off the equivalent of a Scottish win over Brazil at football or New Zealand at rugby.

Great Britain were in the final.

Ironically those same Swiss who had done team GB such a favour earlier were Martin's final opponents.

As we all now know, a staggering BBC1 Network audience of 5.7 million people tuned in to see if Great Britain could win their first Winter Olympic Gold since Torvill and Dean 18 years before.

And Rhona Martin's victory could not have been more dramatic. After 13 matches and more than 35 hours of intense competition, it all came down to one final stone and a margin of error of no more than a few millimetres. It was, as I called it in commentary, "a stone for glory". It was Rhona's last chance; her moment – and she took it, quite brilliantly.

It was the very essence of what sport is all about. And that is why, amidst all the other Olympics, Commonwealth Games, World Cups, Open Championships and Cup Finals I have enjoyed, Rhona Martin's golden moment in Salt Lake City is my greatest sporting memory of all.

JOHN DOUGLAS
Former back row player of the Scotland rugby scrum in the early 1960s

Having been extremely lucky fitness-wise through a successful International Rugby career, I have great sympathy for Norrie McArthur's plight and his support for his charity the Scottish Motor Neurone Disease Association.

I took up golf at the age of 30 years.

Still playing rugby, I had only 3 summer months to play before serious training started yet again.

My target was to break 90 in my first season, which I achieved on Gullane No. 2 with a long putt for an 89.

I adjourned to the most popular hostelry for some beer.

In comes Double Internationalist (Rugby and Cricket for Scotland) and newspaper reporter Norman Mair, accompanied by three very famous Hibernian Scottish international footballers (Lawrie Reilly, Eddie Turnbull and wee Bobby Johnstone ... all 3 handicap.

Passing by the elated JD he asked how I had fared.

"Great, Norman, I shot an 89."

"John, John ... you shoot a 69, you *accumulate* an 89."

A deflated JD; but it was used by Norman in an introduction to an Open Programme to show how handicapping in golf can give everyone pleasure.

GREG DYKE
Director-General of the BBC

My best sporting moment was in May '99 when Manchester United beat Bayern Munich to win the UEFA Champions League. I was at the stadium in Barcelona and like all United fans had given up when Sheringham and Solskjaer gave United the match. Two minutes never to be forgotten.

DR WINIFRED M EWING
MSP for the Highlands and Islands of Scotland, President of the Scottish National Party

I was a member of the Glasgow University swimming team from 1946 to 1951. We annually swam against Belfast University and the two Dublin Universities. I was finally swimming in the Women's Team Race and gained a victory for the team against all three in 1950.

I believe swimming is the best sport. Footballers end up with sore knee joints, as do long-distance runners like my husband who has had two knee replacements.

Swimming is good for everyone.

BRUCE FORSYTH, OBE
Entertainer

My most memorable "personal" sporting occasion was when I got a hole in one at White Webbs Golf Club (Enfield, London), and believe it or not, I was on my own! The nearest thing to me was a dog that was more interested in the tree he was christening, than my elation at the time.

Another memorable occasion was when I got to meet that terrific American comic Bob Newhart and play some golf with him at the Las Vegas International Golf Club. Tony Newley's drummer, a croupier, and that wonderful American singer Jack Jones were also present, walking around with us as we played. At a short hole, I hit a very nice shot that bounced just in front of the hole and then dropped right into it. *Well!* We all went crazy and Jack Jones, who is usually a very laid-back guy jumped six feet into the air!

What a shot! So, having got a hole in one, I had to buy a round of drinks for everyone in the club house. In that club, however, nothing was paid for in cash. Everything was paid for in coupons, so Bob, as the member, had to pay for the drinks. Wasn't that nice of him? A hole in one, but no hole in my wallet!

URI GELLER
World-famous mystic, and chairman of Exeter City Football Club

In May 2002 I became the Co-Chairman of Exeter City FC, an unassuming yet rather charming little club in the Third Division, located in the enchanting surrounds of Devon. Now, to me it came as no surprise that I found myself taking over this club, and I'll tell you why.

The story begins in 1996, when my then 15-year-old son Daniel suddenly started supporting Exeter City, who are known as the Grecians. Daniel's passion for the City was as immense as it was bizarre. Why on earth would he choose to follow a team who are based 200 miles from his home?! Well, I soon began to notice that this was no random decision. Daniel felt an incredible attachment to the area and a love for the club that I'd never seen him display towards anything before. I was convinced that his attraction to the city of Exeter and its struggling football team was more than an odd happening, something deeper and more meaningful – synchronicity!

On our very first visit to the place, Daniel seemed to instantly recognise the streets and buildings and even managed to navigate us along the hidden roads until we reached the quaint football ground. On this balmy summer evening, Exeter City were taking on Premiership glamour-boys Chelsea, whose star-studded side had just swollen a little more with their signing of Italian striker Gianluca Vialli. The world's media focused all their attention on the London giants and here they were at Exeter City's St James's Park!

The 10,000-strong crowd crammed into the stadium were anticipating and expecting a real rollicking by Ruud Gullit's Blues. As the game unfolded, it became clear that the script was going to have to be re-written. Division Three minnows, City (who incidentally went on to finish 22nd in the league that season, just escaping relegation into the Conference) had not only given Chelsea a run for their money, they had only gone and won the game 2–1!!

The excitement, jubilation, joy and delight expressed vivaciously and vociferously by the red-and-white contingent, who had really turned up in their hordes had to be seen to be believed. The mighty Chelsea had been defeated, assuring City probably their best-ever pre-season result. Needless to say, I had been sitting there quietly, concentrating like mad every time a City player had the ball, willing them silently to shoot and score. It must have worked subconsciously!

That was the first step of Daniel's and my journey that led us to acquiring the club he adores. His love affair began, there and then, on that momentous night, and you can imagine his immeasurable happiness and pride when he became the Co-vice-chairman of his beloved team.

Now that we are a little bigger in stature (superstar and close friend Michael Jackson is an Honorary Director!) we are plotting our next scalp – winning the Division Three Championship!

RICHARD GORDON
BBC Scotland sports correspondent

So many memories, it's difficult to pin one down, but I'd probably go for Raith Rovers' incredible run between November '94 and November '95.

Their penalties-win over Celtic in the Coca Cola Cup Final was definitely the most dramatic, most thrilling Final I've ever attended. That of course qualified them for the UEFA Cup, and Chick Young and I followed them throughout that campaign, a campaign which, for us, included a day-trip to Iceland.

Having won 3–1 in the home leg, Rovers were overrun by Akranes in the second leg but, thanks to goalkeeper Scott Thompson's heroics, escaped with a 1–0 defeat. Next up came the mighty Bayern Munich – the home leg was switched to Easter Road and a 2–0 defeat looked to have ended Raith's hopes, but at half-time in the return, Jimmy Nicholl's men led 1–0 in the Olympic Stadium. Bayern eventually came out on top, but Raith emerged with great credit and it was, all in all, a fantastic adventure for all of us lucky enough to have shared in it.

ALAN GREEN
BBC radio sports commentator

My favourite sporting memory is of Great Britain's coxless four winning Olympic gold in Sydney. I was there, commentating, but I had come to consider Steven Redgrave, Matthew Pinsent, James Cracknell and Tim Foster my friends, as well as representatives of the country, and got to know them really well in the build-up.

On the big day, I was more emotional than at any other time in my working life. So emotional that, as the race approached, I worried that I might be too emotional to do the job. I remember digging my pen hard into the palm of my hand. It hurt! But it was effective in helping me to calm down.

ROBIN HARPER
MSP for the Lothians, Scottish Green Party

When I was at Aberdeen University in 1954, I was a member of the cross-country team and also liked the odd game of rugby with the (drinking) 3rd XV. One Saturday I was promoted to the 2nd XV. I turned up to find that the opposition, Robert Gordon's, were two men short. As I had never scored for the 3rd XV and never played for the seconds before, they were only too happy to volunteer me to play for Gordon's and hoped that this would improve Aberdeen's chances of winning the match.

I won the match for Gordon's in the last five minutes with a superb try, running from inside our own half, via a one-two with their fly half. The moment is still fresh in my memory.

GAVIN HASTINGS
Former Scotland rugby captain

Living in the home of golf and having played the game since about the age of 6 or 7, I remember being in St Andrews for a summer holiday with my family a few years later. My Dad then took my older brother and me for a game on the Old Course and aged 14, I can't remember too much about the round except to say that it was memorable for the finish.

Standing on the 18th tee, I checked my score and worked out that I needed a four at the last to break 100. I smacked a drive away just short of the road that crosses the 1st and 18th fairway, Granny Clark's Wynd, but "duffed" my second just short of Valley of Sin. A chip up to about 4ft was pretty good, given the circumstances and, as I waited for the crucial putt, I couldn't help noticing the spectators that you always get around the 18th green.

I walked nervously to my marker and replaced the ball before having a good look at its line. The thought of Doug Sanders and that "missed putt" was put to the back of my mind and somehow I got the ball into the hole for a 99. I was well chuffed, and my Dad was chuffed for me, and my brother less so, as I had seen him off.

I have played that hole many times since. I managed to birdie it during last year's Dunhill Links Championship but that four will remain with me for as long as I am playing golf.

SCOTT HASTINGS
Scotland and British Lions rugby player

Tale 1:
My favourite sporting memory is when Scotland won the Grand Slam in 1990 beating England at Murrayfield on 17th March 1990 by 13 points to 7. Both teams were playing for a "Winner takes all" show down. There was the Calcutta Cup, The Triple Crown, The Five Nations championship and the Grand Slam to play for. Kenny Milne Scotland's hooker advised the BBC in a pre-match interview that he hoped Scotland would win at least one of the titles!

Tale 2:
Following the above game the SRU organised a celebration dinner in the company of HRH The Princess Royal. During the dinner I went up to Princess Anne and asked her for the microphone. In front of the team and 200 others I said "Excuse me ma'am but there is one question that has not been answered ... Jenny Ovens will you marry me?"

Luckily she said yes and we have two wonderful kids and 12 years of marriage behind us.

ROY HATTERSLEY
Member of the House of Lords and writer

As a boy who played cricket – enthusiastically but not very well – in Yorkshire after the war, my great hero was Len Hutton. For years I chased him round the country in

Sir Leonard Hutton   © PA Photo

the unsuccessful hope of getting his autograph and thought that I batted like him because I gave my cap a neurotic twitch after every ball.

In 1989, on the Saturday morning of the test match between England and Pakistan, I was queuing up to pay my bill in the Queens' Hotel, Leeds, when I noticed that Sir Leonard Hutton was immediately in front of me. He turned round and, to my delight, said, "Are you back in England now or are you still coaching in Tasmania?" After I stuttered that he had got it wrong, he offered to take me to the ground.

So here I am, a man of few achievements, but number amongst them the privilege of being driven to a test match by Sir Leonard Hutton.

DENNIS HEALEY
Rt. Hon. Lord Healey of Riddlesden CH MBE

My most memorable sports occasion was as a spectator at an event at Headingley, Leeds. Don Bradman caught a ball almost on the boundary line about 10 feet from where I was sitting!

It was a great occasion!

Donald Bradman, far left, an Australian cricketing great
© Scottish Daily Record

PAUL HEGARTY
Manager and former captain of Dundee United

I was fortunate to play in many memorable and important games for Dundee United.

To play and captain the club and win the Premier League in season 1982/83 was my greatest achievement in my football career.

The final game was against our local rivals Dundee at Dens Park. Winning and clinching the game and cham-

Dundee United, Premier League winners 1982/83
© Scottish Daily Record

pionship was a remarkable achievement in the club's history after playing ten months of skill, hard work, courage and luck to land the biggest prize in Scottish football.

It was a privilege to play with some very fine players and to give our loyal fans something they will never forget!

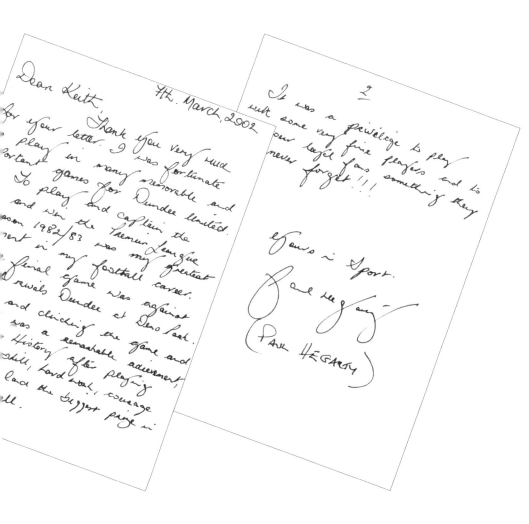

KATE HOEY
MP and former Sports minister

I have many sporting memories. Watching the coxless four win the Gold Medal in Sydney at the 2000 Olympics was quite special but probably the most memorable will, for me, always be seeing Joey Dunlop win the Formula One race at the Isle of Man TT in June 2000.

At 48, he showed he was still the King of the Road. It was made more memorable because he was from the same county in Northern Ireland as myself and I garlanded him after his victory. It was the first time a sports minister had attended a TT.

Of course, the event was made even more poignant when, a few weeks later, Joey was killed in an obscure race in Estonia.

MIKE INGHAM
BBC radio football correspondent

It's a bit corny, but what stands out for me as my favourite sporting memory is being taken to the FA Cup final, for the first time, by my dad.

Having found out only the night before that he had got tickets, we went by train from Derby, where we lived, to see Preston North End take on West Ham in 1964. We were neutrals on that occasion but stood at the Preston end, next to a couple of their fans, one of whom was doing a commentary on the match.

After 15 minutes or so, I looked across and saw that his companion's eyes were directed up to the sky and I realised that he was blind.

From that moment I understood the value of commentary.

HAZEL IRVINE
BBC sports correspondent

My favourite sporting memory is from the 1980 Moscow Olympics when Scotland's Allan Wells sprinted to gold in the 100 metres. I was 15 at the time and was already keen on athletics. But his dedication, his single-minded determination and ultimately his triumph fuelled my love of sport.

Seven years later I met Allan when auditioning for a presentation job on the 1988 Seoul Olympics during which I was required to interview him. What an opportunity to pose all of the questions I'd always wanted to ask!

In no small part due to Allan, I got the job!

MUSTAFA (MUZZY) IZZET
Turkey and Leicester City midfielder

From a personal point of view, an important moment for me was Steve Claridge's last-minute goal for Leicester in the 1996 play-off final against Crystal Palace at Wembley.

That took us into the Premiership, where every footballer dreams of playing.

More generally, I'm a big boxing fan and the memory that stands out is of Sugar Ray Leonard coming out of retirement to beat Marvin Hagler.

Muzzy Izzet   © Scottish Daily Record

JIM JEFFERIES
Manager, Kilmarnock Football Club

My most memorable moment in football is without a doubt the Scottish Cup Final in May 1998 when Hearts won against Rangers, 2–1 at Celtic Park.

I was very proud to be manager of Hearts at that time and it is a memory that will live with me forever.

Heart of Midlothian, Scottish Cup Final winners 1998
© Scottish Daily Record

THE KILMARNOCK FOOTBALL CLUB LTD.

Secretary
KEVIN COLLINS

REGISTERED IN SCOTLAND NUMBER
GROUND & REGISTERED OFFICE

RUGBY PARK
KILMARNOCK KA1 2DP

TEL. NO.
FAX NO.

Manager
JIM JEFFERIES

8th March 2002

Keith McCartney
The Waid Academy
Anstruther
Fife
KY10 3HD

Dear Keith

My most memorable moment in football is without a doubt the Scottish Cup Final in May 1998 when Hearts won against Rangers, 2-1 at Celtic Park. I was very proud to be Manager of Hearts at that time and it is a memory that will live with me for ever.

Yours sincerely

Jim Jefferies
MANAGER

Manchester City Plc

KK/JMcC

26th March 2002

Mr Keith McCartney
The Waid Academy

Maine Road Moss Side
Manchester M14 7WN
T.
F.
E. mcfc@mcfc.co.uk
W. www.mcfc.co.uk

Dear Keith

Thank you for your letter asking me to describe my most memorable sporting occasion.

It was my last game for Liverpool in 1977 in Rome in the European Cup Final when we beat Borussia Munchengladbach 3-1.

Not only was it my last game after many successful years at Liverpool but I was leaving the club to play professional football in Germany for SV Hamburg. As you can imagine it was both memorable and ironic under the circumstances.

Good luck with your very worthy fund raising efforts for SMNDA.

Kind regards

Kevin Keegan
Manager

Chairman, D.A.Bernstein
Directors, C.M. Bird // B. Bodek // A.M. Lewis // A.J. Mackintosh // D. Tueart // J.C. Wardle
General Secretary, J.B. Halford

Registered in England. Registered No.

EIDOS

le coq sportif

KEVIN KEEGAN
Manager, Manchester City

My most memorable sporting occasion was my last game for Liverpool in 1977 in Rome in the European Cup Final when we beat Borussia Munchengladbach 3–1.

Not only was it my last game after many successful years at Liverpool but also I was leaving the club to play professional football in Germany for SV Hamburg. As you can imagine it was both memorable and ironic under the circumstances.

Kevin Keegan   © Scottish Daily Record

SIR ROBIN KNOX-JOHNSTON
Round-the-world sailor

A close friend of mine got married, and arranged to have his honeymoon in Bermuda so that it coincided with a world championship in which he stood a good chance.

He set out for the first race, dropped his bride on a convenient rock well clear of the coast where she could watch the racing, and became immersed in his racing.

At the end of the day, having done quite well, he sailed back with the fleet, hauled his boat ashore, unrigged it, and went to the bar to join the other competitors.

About an hour later someone asked him where his bride was.

Yes, the poor girl was still sitting on the rock!

JOHN LAMBIE
Manager of Partick Thistle football club

My most memorable sporting occasion was playing against the great Ghento at the Bernabeu Stadium. Real Madrid beat St Johnstone 2–1.

Others include scoring a hat trick in 1953, beating Blackburn RC 4–1 in the school final and bringing the Ross Cup back to Whitburn for the first time.

John Lambie   © Scottish Daily Record

PAUL LAWRIE
Golfer

The Open Championship, Carnoustie 1999 was fantastic and the highlight of my career so far. Winning The Open Championship is every golfer's dream.

The golf I really enjoy is Open Championship-type links test. I love bumping it in there. 150 to the pin into a howling gale, you're going to hit a 2-iron off your back foot.

I have a replica Claret jug that sits in my golf room and when I'm in there, hitting balls or putting, I take it down and look at the names when I have a five-minute break – it's just awesome.

JIM LEIGHTON

Ex Aberdeen, Manchester United, Hibernian and Scotland goalkeeper

The best moment of my sporting career was when Scotland played Brazil at the opening match of the World Cup in France in 1998.

Jim Leighton   © Scottish Daily Record

Everything about the experience was special: being involved in the magic of the opening ceremony, playing the World Champions at the time, playing in the new stadium which was full to capacity. I had been left out of the picture for the Euro 96 competition so coming back to play in my fourth World Cup Finals at that stage in my career was something else.

It was my proudest moment.

JIM LEISHMAN
Livingston Football Club director and team manager

I've enjoyed a few memorable moments in football, both as a player and a manager, but I think the greatest thrill of my playing career came in 1972 when I faced Rangers at Ibrox for the first time.

It was a fantastic game and, with the score at 3–3, I took the ball in the inside-right position and beat two Rangers defenders before finding the net with a left-footed shot which gave Dunfermline a 4–3 victory.

As I said, that was in 1972, but, to date, it remains the last winning goal ever recorded by a Dunfermline player at Ibrox – and that it was scored against the same Rangers team who went on to win the European Cup Winners Cup that year made it all the more memorable.

Jim Leishman   ©Scottish Daily Record

HELEN LIDDELL
Secretary of State for Scotland

My most memorable sporting experience was asking Kenny Dalglish if he was interested in football!

RT. HON. HELEN LIDDELL MP

HOUSE OF COMMONS
LONDON SW1A 0AA

Mr Keith McCartney
Waid Academy

19 March 2002

Dear Keith

Thank you very much for your letter of 7 March 2002.

My most memorable sporting experience was asking Kenny Dalgleish if he was interested in football!

Best wishes.

Yours sincerely

Helen Liddell

Rt Hon Helen Liddell MP

All correspondence to:

Constituency Office

Perhaps Kenny Dalglish's favourite sporting moment was meeting Mrs Liddell?

SEAN LINEEN
New Zealand-born Scotland rugby player

My favourite memory was touring with Scotland to New Zealand in 1990 after we had won the Grand Slam. It was North champions versus South champions and we played some superb rugby and the backs managed to wrestle the ball away from the forwards for a change and play more of a 15-man game. I got a chance to drink some decent beer (amateur days were good) and be part of a very special group of players. Two memories stick with me from that tour.

The first is scoring a try against the All Blacks, it was a move we had worked on and I scored under the posts. As

Sean Lineen   © Scottish Daily Record

95

I was running back, Scott Hastings gave me a high five which nearly broke my wrist!

The second involves Gavin Hastings. It was pouring with rain in Auckland for the second test and we were leading the All Blacks which they didn't like and resorted to underhand tactics.

They gave away a penalty 55 metres out and Gav said he could kick it – and he did. Two minutes later their boisterous prop Richard Loe gave away another penalty in the same spot and up stepped Big Gav and kicked it again. The crowd roared their approval.

Outside the tests we went through the tour unbeaten and 14 of us stayed on for an extra four days to further sample the Kiwi hospitality with wine tasting, river rafting through rapids and bungee jumping on the menu.

JONAH LOMU
New Zealand, All Black winger

My best sporting memory was Muhammad Ali beating George Foreman to regain the World Heavyweight title.

GARY LINEKER

Former England, Everton, Leicester, Barcelona and Tottenham footballer

It has to be the Poland match in the 1986 World Cup, because it was just such a life-changing experience for me. I hadn't scored for a while and England were on the verge of a humiliating exit. Then I got a hat-trick, ended up leading scorer in the tournament and got a move to Barcelona. It could all have been so different.

Gary Lineker, 1986 World Cup   © Gordon Fraser/Scottish Daily Record

ELLEN MCARTHUR
Yachtswoman

My last Route de Rhum race in 1998 was really the beginning of my road to the Vendée Globe but it was a nail-biting experience to even get to the start line. We had been struggling to find a suitable boat but eventually were offered an Open 50 called "Great Circle". It was based in Bermuda so I had to fly out there with two crew to deliver her back to France. The day before flying out from Heathrow, we had a meeting with Kingfisher Plc – it proved to be a meeting that would have a big impact on realising my dreams.

A few days later I got the call from Mark to say Kingfisher had agreed to the sponsorship – we were off and now needed to get the boat back in time to re-brand her in the new colours of our sponsor. This proved to be easier said than done – major problems on board needed fixing even before we departed Bermuda and then Hurricane Lisa forced us to return to Bermuda after a few days. We finally made it to the Azores having nursed her across – the sails were literally hanging together. Then Mark called, his first words were: "Are you sitting down?"

My mouth went dry and I immediately thought of everything that might have gone wrong but to my amazement the news was good. Not just good, fantastic! He had managed to charter Pete Goss's 50-foot Aqua Quorum that had competed in the last Vendée Globe – now I knew

I had a strong boat that had proved herself in the harsh Southern Ocean.

As it turned out, she needed to be tough, the first few days of the 1998 Route de Rhum were horrendous. Before we left I had been stunned to see not just the quality of the fleet and competitors in St Malo but the crowds of spectators that poured into the port just to catch a glimpse of the boats and their drivers. The organisers estimate that over a million people visited St Malo in the week running up to the start. For me it was my first real experience of being constantly in the public and media eye. I would feel someone tugging at my jacket and expect to turn round and see someone I knew but it was always a stranger with a big smile, a pen, a piece of paper, asking for an autograph and wishing me "bon chance".

The North Atlantic in November dished out what you would expect and we battled in winds from 35–55 knots. I suffered ripped sails, taking on a colossal amount of water below via the forehatch. Bailing out with a plastic scoop that more often than not lost its contents as we crashed down a wave was a frustrating and humiliating experience.

The worst of all though was the failure of the canting keel. A hydraulic pipe in the keel box had burst. The oil was everywhere. I had to re-fill the 10-litre reservoir using a teaspoon whilst we were still crashing through the waves – it took forever. In the end, I could actually see the comical side of the situation – me laying in the bowels of the boat, covered in oil with various supplies of food sloshing past (my bailing out had not been as effective as I hoped!).

It was a tough, tough race, as I don't doubt it will be again, but I won the Open 50 class and only four Open 60s out of the 12 that started were ahead of me at the finish. So to be on the start line on 9 November will see a full circle completed – I began my Kingfisher adventure back then in 1998 and in the 2002 edition of the race I will be finishing my solo adventure on Kingfisher.

A hard thing to imagine, but the multihulls beckon and for me and Kingfisher this is our future.

NORRIE MCARTHUR

Head of Centre, Waid Centre, Anstruther. Former principal teacher of physical education at the Waid Academy, Anstruther. Former centre forward for Clachnacuddin, Ross County and Elgin City

As a spectator:
I attended PE college at Jordanhill from 1966–69 and was privileged to attend all of the home games in Celtic's European Cup campaign. Parkhead was filled to capacity for these matches and the atmosphere was electric, as was the football served up by the team. I watched the final on a large screen in Glasgow University Union and the streets afterwards were alive with those celebrating a famous victory with an all-Scottish team (and manager). As a lifelong East Fife supporter my European experience was limited!

The 1990 Calcutta Cup and Grand Slam winning Scottish Rugby Team which beat England 13–7 in the final match of the season was also a memorable occasion.

As a participant:
Because I played many sports I have several memorable sporting moments that I look back on with pleasure.

Football
Scoring the only goal of the 1970 North of Scotland Cup Final for Ross County v Elgin City at Kingsmill Park – home of Inverness Thistle and now a housing estate.

Norrie McArthur, in white, playing for Clachnacuddin against Ross County, 1973
Photograph courtesy of Norrie McArthur

Playing for Elgin City against Aberdeen FC at Pittodrie in season 1970/71 in the third round of the Scottish Cup. Aberdeen were the current holders and, being a local derby, the ground was packed with over 24,000 spectators. 2–0 down at half time, we eventually lost 3 goals in the last 17 minutes to suffer a 5–0 defeat but a wonderful experience, having beaten Stenhousemuir (A) and Berwick Rangers (H) in the first and second rounds.

The following season, being in the Elgin City side which lost to Kilmarnock at Elgin (1–4) in front of 10,500 spectators having beaten Stenhousemuir (H) and Burntisland Shipyard (A) in previous rounds.

Golf
Recording my only hole in one at the 159 yard, par 3, 16th hole at Crail Balcomie on Sunday, September 23, 1979, using an eight iron.

Cricket
Scoring my one and only century (102 not out) in a Scottish Small Clubs Cup match against Garrowhill on Sunday, 21 May, 1989, playing for Waid FPCC.

Raft racing
Winning the 1985 Kenmore to Aberfeldy race as a member of the Sundancer team – it was my first victory but the team's third in a row. The crowd was over 30,000.
Parachute jump
In tandem with instructor Scotty Milne in June 2001 at

Errol Airfield doing a freefall jump from 13,000 feet with the parachute opening at 5,000 feet – the thrill of a lifetime.

As a manager
Winning seven trophies and a league title at St Andrews United between 1988 to 1991 – the league title was won without losing any of the 30 matches of the 1989/90 season.

FRED MACAULAY
Comedian and BBC Radio Scotland presenter

As someone who hardly played team sports, I've felt in these last few years that I really missed out on the camaraderie. From 1997 to 2000 I co-presented a chat show on BBC with Ally McCoist, the great striker for Rangers and Scotland (and St Johnstone, Sunderland and Kilmarnock, for the sticklers for detail!). Ally was terrific fun to work with and anyone who's heard an after dinner speaker in Scotland at a sportsmen's evening will have heard an Ally McCoist story. Speakers the length and breadth of Scotland would struggle for work if they hadn't encountered "the legend" !

I'm no different.

In 1998 we made a television programme from the Eiffel Tower which was broadcast in Scotland the evening before the Scotland-Brazil game which opened the 1998 World Cup in France. Part of the format of our shows was that Ally and I went onto the streets of whichever town we were visiting to get some *vox pops* from the locals.

In Paris we were looking for comments from members of the Tartan Army, many of whom had been in the city for three or four days getting "acclimatised" for the game!

I have to say that on several occasions during the series we had struggled to get locals to contribute. The Tartan Army were out in force and were only too willing to contribute to our programme. Or so it seemed. On three separate occasions that day I saw our director give us a thumbs-up to say he was pleased with what the lads had said and to stop filming. When the cameras stopped rolling, the Scots had the last word saying: "Here, you can't broadcast that, by the way ... We're on the sick!"

Only a Scottish football supporter would have the gall to phone in sick two days before the World Cup started!

But my own personal memory was an incident at our hotel. Ally is renowned for his (poor) timekeeping. How he managed to get onto a pitch at three o'clock on a Saturday all those years is beyond me. We were checking out of our hotel and I phoned his room to see if he was on his way to reception.

"I'm just in the shower, I'll be five minutes, pal!"

I reckoned he might be nearer ten, so I sat in reception with a newspaper. After 40 minutes I phoned his room, and when I asked how close he was to being ready he said ...

"I'm just in the shower, I'll be five minutes, pal!"

I asked if he needed a hand with his packing and he said that he wouldn't mind. I took the lift to his floor and knocked on the door. A rather sheepish Ally appeared at the door, dripping from the shower with only a towel round his waist.

Seconds before I'd got to his door, the chambermaid had knocked. Assuming it was me, Ally had bolted from the shower and flung the door open (minus towel) to greet a rather flabbergasted young French girl. When I arrived, he stuck his head around the door and shouted to the girl: "This is who I thought you were!"

Fortunately for us, the girl hadn't a clue who we were and just went on with her duties, safe in the knowledge that the naked man in room 513's "friend" had arrived!

It was, after all, "gay Paree", but we'd have had some explaining to do to our wives back home if word had got out ... which it now has I suppose!

Ally McCoist, Ewan McGregor and Fred MacAulay in France for the show *McCoist and MacAulay* and for the 1998 World Cup

© SMG Newspapers Ltd

MARGO MACDONALD
Journalist and Scottish Nationalist

One of my most vivid memories is of winning my first ever medal for diving. I was 11 years of age and the competition was the Burgh of Hamilton Championships, held in Hamilton Baths: deep end, six foot eight inches.

That last detail gives a clue as to the tariff rating on each of the dives performed. However, I was the proudest wee girl in Lanarkshire to end up only two points off the woman (18 years of age) who was the established champion of that area of Lanarkshire. As I walked up to be presented with my silver medal I genuinely thought life couldn't get any better than this.

Waiting to shake my hand and hand over the medal were big George Young, then the captain of Rangers and big Jock Stein who was not only the captain of Celtic, but like myself born and bred in Burnbank. (Also the home of Walter McGowan, world boxing champion... but that's another story.)

MURDO MACLEOD
Former Celtic and Scotland player

Well it's a toss up between Celtic and Scotland.

In my first season at Celtic, in 1979, I scored in a 4–2 win at Ibrox against Rangers in the 90th minute.

For Scotland it was my first game in the World Cup. It was in 1990 against Sweden and we won 2–1. McCall and Johnston were the scorers.

Murdo Macleod   © Scottish Daily Record

EDDIE MACGEACHY
Former Principal teacher of PE, Waid Academy

This story goes back to the days when the Railway line ran past the Waid Playing Fields which were used for Rugby, Football, Hockey and Athletics. The train driver uses to sometimes give a "toot" and a wave as the train passed.

During an athletics practice, the javelin once landed on the rail line and the train ran over it and mangled it.

In the mid-1950s young George Doig had been entered for the Scottish Schools' Championships at Edinburgh for the Under 15 Pole Vault. The pole was approximately 11 feet long and made of aluminium so it had to be put in the guard's van as we travelled by train from Anstruther to Edinburgh.

We walked up Waverley Steps and onto Princes Street, hoping to get a tramcar. The boys got onto the tram but the conductor, after consulting with the driver, refused to carry the pole. I knew that there was nothing for it but, in order that George remained fresh, to walk all the way to Goldenacre carrying the pole myself. It was difficult to carry it upright, so I had to carry it horizontally on my shoulder, much to the annoyance of my fellow pedestrians.

It was a long way – approximately two miles. I eventually flagged down a lorry driver who told me that he was not allowed to drive off his route, but in spite of that, he took pity on me and drove George's pole and me on my way to Goldenacre. The next thing that happened was that the lorry broke down, so there was nothing for it but to shoulder the pole and begin walking again.

It all had a happy ending when George Doig came first in the Under 15 Pole Vault and took home the gold Medal, which was presented again at assembly on the Monday morning by Mr Robin, Rector of The Waid Academy.

IAN MCGEECHAN
Scotland Head Coach, Scottish Rugby Union Plc

The occasion that will always live long in my memory took place on March 17, 1990, a day in which preparation and action came together as one.

It started with a very nervous group of people, players and coaches, at the Braid Hills Hotel in Edinburgh. It was strange that the atmosphere was quiet, not over-excited, it was as though everybody involved knew they had the chance and the ability to make history.

I suppose the real memory starts with the bus journey from the hotel to Murrayfield with people applauding on the pavements, holding flags out of windows. There was no doubt that this was a single nation behind one team and it was very clear that this had got through to the players.

The players in their turn wanted to make a statement to every Scot to show that they were there as a real team who meant business. They had decided the previous night to let England go on to the field and wait and walk so that their intent would be obvious to everyone. I still get shivers down my spine when I read about it or think about it but for the first 15 minutes of that game, England didn't win a ball, Scotland were there for real and I think it shocked England to such an extent that they never fully recovered. We had a group of players who created and maintained a momentum throughout the whole 80 minutes. What was truly amazing was the reaction of the crowd that got so close to its team, that it

Flanker Finlay Calder at Murrayfield 1990 © SMG Newspapers Ltd

cheered every single lineout won, never mind any good rugby being played. They realised the edges that were so crucial to stopping England.

Within a game as a coach you are trying to look at tactics and how it is going, whether there are injuries, whether a player is getting tired and obviously how well you think they are going, and after the electric start the roller coaster of emotions changed again, when England scored a try so easily, they just reminded everybody how good and dangerous they were. Having played with the wind in the first half and just built a lead I think everyone expected England just to turn up the pressure but what a way for Scotland to start the second half-scrum, brilliant execution of passes, a kick, a chase, and a try and England were back on their heels once more – and for Scotland there was no looking back. I don't think I have seen any group of players harass and chase and close space as quickly as that group of players did for the remaining 35 minutes.

I also remember a stunning tackle by Scott Hastings on Rory Underwood when it looked as though the flying wing could have been away, but apart from that, it was England striving to create things under extreme pressure.

Eventually having played nearly 3 minutes of injury time, England's last move petered out into touch no more than 20 metres from the Scottish line, but that was it. When the referee blew his whistle, the feeling that ran through everybody was quite unbelievable. The players, the crowd, every supporter, knew they had been part of something which will remain very, very special. I understand the score was even relayed to the customers in Jenners department store in Edinburgh city centre and even there it got a cheer.

What followed was our international dinner and, again, strangely enough, it was not over-exuberant but just a very enjoyable evening where I think everybody wanted to soak-in the whole day's event.

There is no better feeling and sometimes no greater achievement than when a group of people are working in total harmony.

ALEX MCLEISH
Manager, Rangers Football Club

My favourite sporting event was all the more memorable due to the fact that I participated in it!

The 1983 European Cup Winners Cup Final against the "Mighty" Real Madrid! My team was of course Aberdeen FC. It was a remarkable achievement for a small provincial club to take on and defeat arguably the most famous club in the world.

Mark McGhee of Aberdeen FC   © Scottish Daily Record

Victory was ours thanks to goals by Eric Black and John Hewitt. Juanito replied for Real from the penalty spot. On the night, however there's no doubt the best team won. (A team consisting only of homegrown Scots players by the way!)

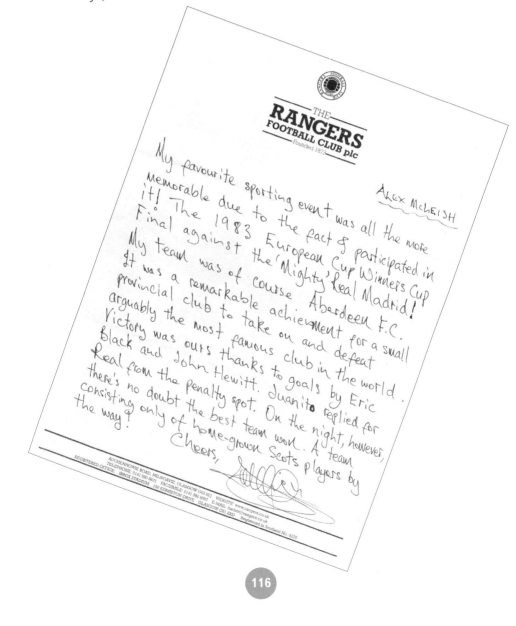

THE RANGERS FOOTBALL CLUB plc
Founded 1873

ALEX McLEISH

My favourite sporting event was all the more memorable due to the fact I participated in it! The 1983 European Cup Winners Cup Final against the 'Mighty' Real Madrid!

My team was of course Aberdeen F.C. It was a remarkable achievement for a small provincial club to take on and defeat arguably the most famous club in the world. Victory was ours thanks to goals by Eric Black and John Hewitt. Juanito replied for Real from the penalty spot. On the night, however, there's no doubt the best team won. A team consisting only of home-grown Scots players by the way!

Cheers,

REGISTERED OFFICE: IBROX STADIUM, 150 EDMISTON DRIVE, GLASGOW G51 2XD. Registered in Scotland No. 4276
AUCHENHOWIE ROAD, MILNGAVIE, GLASGOW G62 6EJ. WEBSITE www.rangers.co.uk
TELEPHONE: 0141 580 8631. FACSIMILE: 0141 586 8887. E-MAIL ibrox@rangers.co.uk

HENRY MCLEISH
MSP for Fife Central

When I was 12 years of age (in 1960) I was fortunate enough to attend probably the greatest football match the world has ever seen. This was the European Cup Final involving Real Madrid and Eintracht at Hampden Park, Glasgow. The crowd was a staggering 141,000. Eintracht had beaten Glasgow Rangers 12–4 on aggregate in the semi-finals but were beaten by Real Madrid in the final by a margin of 7–3. The football was simply the best I have ever seen and was a bit like watching the Harlem Globetrotters. Individual ball skills and superb goals. I think Puskas scored 4 and DiStefano scored 3. I was truly privileged to watch such skills, so much so that even in my fast approaching older years I can still remember the victorious Real Madrid side, which was Dominguez, Marchitos, Pachin, Vidal, Santamaria, Zarraga, Canario, DelSol, DiStefano, Puskas and Ghento – what a game.

I was 18 years of age (in 1966) and playing for East Fife when I was asked to join the Scottish professional youth squad to travel to Yugoslavia for a mini World Cup. The tournament was held in Pristina, now of course capital of Kosovo. I played in the second game against Holland and still have my Scottish jersey and Scottish badge as a memento of this fantastic occasion. We drew 1–1, as indeed was the result in all our games. We did not qualify for the quarter finals. You can imagine the sense of

Former East Fife footballer Henry McLeish shows his ball skills
© Scottish Daily Record

pride and honour to be playing for your country on foreign soil. This feeling was only slightly undermined when we stood at the start of the game to hear the national anthems. We were anticipating the playing of "Scotland the Brave". Alas, they did not have this recording but instead played "The Island of Dreams" by the Springfields!

When I was 15 years of age (in 1963) I left school and signed for Leeds United on a 2-year professional contract. This was in the 1962/63 season when Don Revie took over as manager of that great club. Leeds United were in the Second Division at that time but were promoted in Don Revie's first year. They then went on to become one of the giants of English football. This was the first time I had met Don Revie. He was a great Manager and a great help to all the young players he had recruited. To be signed by such a great Club was a huge personal achievement. I had been brought up in Methil and Kennoway and had done nothing except kick a football up until I was aged 15. This was a memorable occasion for me but it is also quite poignant because Don Revie much later in life developed Motor Neurone Disease.

THE VERY REVEREND DR. ANDREW MCLELLAN
Former Moderator of the General Assembly of the Church of Scotland

Although he had never had an opportunity to see the American golfer in the flesh or on television, Gene Sarazen had been a boyhood hero of my father's. When I was young I heard his name often. Three stories were always told of Sarazen: he invented the sand-wedge, he won all four "majors", and he holed a terrific shot with a four-wood which brought him victory in the US masters – "the shot heard round the world". My father thought he was great.

As an old man, Sarazen competed in the Open Championship at Troon. By chance, I saw a few holes on television one day sitting with my father, just the two of us. At the difficult short eighth hole, the "Postage Stamp", Sarazen did the impossible – he holed in one, live on television. He was 71 years old.

It was a golden moment for me. To see anyone hit a hole in one is very special: but that it should be Gene Sarazen at such an age and in the Open Championship made it extraordinary. And that it brought such extravagant delight to my father sitting beside me – I will never forget it!

DAVID MCLETCHIE
MSP for the Lothians

My most memorable sporting occasion was the 1998 Scottish Cup Final. As a dedicated Hearts fan, our 2–1 victory over Rangers ended a 36 year famine during which time we had won not a single trophy. During that period Hearts fans had experienced many bitter disappointments and frustrations – defeats in the Scottish Cup Finals of 1968, 1976, 1986 and 1996, the loss of two league titles in 1965 and 1986 on goal average and goal difference to Kilmarnock and Celtic respectively and many other disappointments too painful to recall.

The 1998 Cup Final was played at Celtic Park, as Hampden was being restored. It was a beautiful sunny day and was the culmination of the season in which Hearts had been in sparkling league form. All of us felt that a cup win was more than deserved but we were up against a Rangers team under Walter Smith's charge as a manager for the last time and desperate to win the last trophy of the season. With me at the game were my son James, wife Sheila and a group of friends with whom I had attended hundreds of Hearts games over the previous 30 years. What transpired turned out to be the most stressful and emotional and ultimately wonderful sporting day of my life.

Hearts got off to the best possible start with a goal from the penalty spot in the first minute expertly taken by Colin Cameron (sadly now with Wolves). Television replays later indicated that the foul might well have been outside the box but for once it seemed we were to be given the benefit of the doubt and the break of ball from a referee in an important game. The remainder of the first half was a fairly dour affair with relatively few changes being created by either side. On the resumption of play, Hearts unbelievably scored again about an hour through our French centre forward Stephane Adam. At 2–0 up with less than half an hour of play it would seem that it would finally be our day, but few Hearts fans were complacent given the experiences of the past.

Our worst fears were confirmed when McCoist and Durrant combined for McCoist to score an excellent goal which was a prelude to a desperate siege for the last 15 minutes. Rangers were denied what seemed a clear penalty for a foul on McCoist, which the referee Willie Young very generously interpreted as having occurred outside the box by contrast with his earlier penalty decision in Hearts' favour.

Every Hearts fan in the stadium was kicking every ball and willing the referee to whistle for full time. If the game had gone on much longer we would have ended up in intensive care with coronaries such was the level of tension. But at long last the whistle sounded, the team had held on to win and there was a quite an incredible outpouring of joy from the Hearts fans. To their great credit, the Rangers fans were generous in their applause even though the result was a bitter disappointment for them.

It was perfect day – when will I see its like again?

FRANK MCLINTOCK
Former Arsenal captain

Winning the Fairs Cup in 1970 by beating Anderlecht 3–0 at Highbury after we'd lost the first leg 3–1 was a great moment. It was the platform we needed to go on and win the League. Beating Spurs at White Hart Lane to secure the League was another great night, with 40,000 fans locked outside. By the time we'd won the Double at Wembley I was too exhausted to enjoy it fully.

Arsenal versus Anderlecht, 1970 © Scottish Daily Record

BILLY MCNEILL

Former Celtic centre-half, captain and manager. Former captain of Scotland, capped on 29 occasions

My most memorable sporting occasion was when Celtic won the European cup on 25th May 1967 in Lisbon against Inter Milan. Inter were a very strong favourite, and few people gave us very much chance of creating an upset.

Inter started the game confidently and went in front by a penalty scored by Mazzola.

We then started to dominate the game and put Inter under intense pressure. Bobby Murdoch and Bertie Auld had control of mid-field, Jimmy Johnstone was running riot on the right wing and we were creating chances galore. Sarti, the Inter goalkeeper, had a tremendous game and made save after save.

Half time came and we commenced the second half in very positive form. However, Sarti continued his good form and despite hitting the woodwork several times, Inter were still in front. However Tommy Gemmell hit one of his specials and we were level. Despite there only being a short time left I could feel it in my bones that we were going to win and sure enough Stevie Chalmers deflected Bobby Murdoch's shot into the net and Inter were beaten.

The excitement of the fans was matched by the players and the rest is history.

Billy McNeill   © Scottish Daily Record

GEORGE MAKEY, MBE
Founder of Keepers of the Green

This is the story of a memorable sporting moment in the life of Seve Ballesteros and also of mine!

In 1975 I started a golfing "crusade" with just 15 guys who offered their support as I founded Golf Fanatics International, under the heading of my Golf Masters Anonymous to provide powered wheelchairs for disabled children around the UK.

That first tournament of GFI involved 15 of us who each chipped in £25 to cover the cost of the powered wheelchair (PWC) presented on 15th June 1975 to a girl who suffered from cerebral palsy, Paula Marfell, aged 9. Despite a horrendous thunderstorm, the day was a wonderful success with the 16 guys all declaring that I had to do this again.

I developed the theme and presented the first ever powered wheelchair at an Open Championship at Turnberry in 1977 and gradually developed a relationship with some of the world professionals.

Having spoken and written about the "magical" independence, that a disabled child discovers in a PWC – I introduced what I called my "Panel of Magicians"! These were some of the world pros who readily accepted my invitation to make the commitment to donate three PWCs if they won the Open Championship, two if they came second, and one if third.

This was in 1983 when Seve Ballesteros was the first

professional I approached. He readily signed the commitment form and said "I win – I give 10".

On my "panel" I also had Greg Norman, Bernhard Langer, Lee Trevino and Nick Faldo. In the 1983 Open Championship at Royal Birkdale, Seve was winning the Open with just 6 holes to go – but he blew it and Tom Watson won. I met Seve as he came off the 18th green and imagined that he might just brush me aside in the moment of his defeat but no, he came up to me and quietly said: "I'm sorry George but I help you next year". None of my "panel" were in the first 3 that year.

In 1984, the Open Championship was back at St Andrews and Seve was now being regarded as a world champion and attracted huge galleries at St Andrews. He quickly responded to the challenge of the Old Course and certainly set the pace. This was going to be Seve's year. Playing the final hole he was in the lead and he strode up the famous Tom Morris hole to tumultuous applause. I was keyed-up thinking of the 10 powered wheelchairs Seve had promised to give if he won the Open Championship.

Seve holed the winning putt, and, as he punched the air with all his Spanish bravado, the world cheered him loudly. After all the formalities of the trophy presentation, I approached him. He put up his arms and said to the nearby admirers and said: "This is George, the powered wheelchair man. I am going to give 10." He said that he would like to give five to Scottish children and five to English children. In that discussion, we agreed that he would present them at the European Championship to be played at Sunningdale in the September.

I persuaded British Airways to fly five needy youngsters from Fife with their families and helpers and I arranged transport for the party from Heathrow to Sunningdale.

Panasonic, the sponsors of the European Championship, provided a party reception for the ten recipients and the presentation was recorded on video. It truly was a magical occasion with Seve spending several minutes with each youngster.

For Seve this was a very moving experience as he explained to the large gathering of spectators just how happy he was to be able to brighten these needy young lives.

For Seve and the youngsters and their families this was truly a magical sporting occasion with Seve putting something back into this wonderful game at the pinnacle of his playing career.

For me – it was a very special experience in my golfing "crusade".

PROMOTING THE TRADITIONS OF THE GAME OF GOLF AND PROVIDING POWERED MOBILITY FOR THE NEEDY

KEEPERS OF THE GREEN

Founded in 1995 by George Makey MBE · Charity No: CAF Registered Charity

Email: · Web: · Tel./Fax.

THE FIRST EVER GOLFING TRIBUTE TO OLD TOM MORRIS

D.A.Corstorphine Esq.,
The Waid Academy,
Anstruther,
Fife KY10 3HD.

4th.September 2002

Dear D.A.

Mike Ciesla suggested that I might be able to give you a sporting story for inclusion in your commendable book in support of the Scottish Motor Neurone Disease Association and I hope that the enclosed may be worth a mention !

I wish you well in your ongoing endeavours !

Yours sincerely,

(GEORGE MAKEY M.B.E.)., Founder Keeper 'KEEPERS OF THE GREEN'

encl.

Founder: George Makey MBE,
Keeper of the Clubs: Barry Kerr,
Keeper of the Archives: Peter Crabtree,

Patron: David Joy

DIEGO MARADONA
Former captain of Argentina

I find it hard to describe, but the best I can do is to say that it's like touching the sky with your hands. To be able to lift the World Cup for your country is something special. I have played in many places around the world, but the Azteca in Mexico City, where I held up that trophy in 1986, is something that I remember in every detail. I can recall every moment. The occasion is still brilliant in my mind.

MICHAEL MARTIN
Speaker of the House of Commons

I think, like every other Scot, I was extremely proud of the curling champions who won the gold medal at the Winter Olympics in Salt Lake City. It was absolutely marvellous to see the ladies win gold not only for Scotland but the whole of the United Kingdom. That spectacle will always remain with me for many years to come.

The Speaker

Speaker's House   Westminster   London   SW1A 0AA

15 March 2002

Dear Keith,

Thank you for your letter of 7 March asking me to describe my most memorable sporting occasion, either as a player or a spectator.

I have never been a very good sportsman and therefore I can only convey my thoughts as a spectator. I think, like every other Scot, I was extremely proud of the curling champions who won the gold medal at the Winter Olympics in Salt Lake City. It was absolutely marvellous to see the ladies win gold not only for Scotland but the whole of the United Kingdom. That spectacle will always remain with me for many years to come.

Yours

Speaker

Keith McCartney Esq
The Waid Academy

BRIAN MONTEITH
MSP for Mid Scotland and Fife

I had the misfortune to attend Portobello High School which, because it was in the Guinness Book of Records as the Secondary School with most pupils (2,500) had more than its fair share of great sportsmen. This meant I had no chance of playing in the first XI at football or the first XV at rugby. I was slight and fast but was decidedly shortsighted. This meant that when I played for the Porty Thirds I famously ran with the oval ball up the wing and dived heroically for a try, only to find it was the opposition's 22-yard line.

The soccer team was full of schoolboy international caps so the best I could do was play for the staff against the school team! My finest moment was playing as centre-forward and back-heeling a lay-off to my English teacher who ran on and thumped it into the net – against my schoolmates.

Nothing however, beats coaching my two sons at football, one of whom, Duncan, lifted the Under Thirteens Scottish Cup at Hampden last year and now plays for Scotland, and the other, Callum, who reached the Scotland trials and has a sweet right foot.

RAY MONTGOMERIE
Former captain of Kilmarnock Football Club

My most memorable sporting occasion, surprise, surprise, was the Scottish Cup Final on 24th May 1997 when I captained Kilmarnock FC to a 1–0 victory over Falkirk FC. The day will live on in my mind because of the joy it brought through a lot of people in and around Kilmarnock.

Winners of the 1997 Scottish Cup Final, Kilmarnock FC
© Scottish Daily Record

DESMOND MORRIS
Author and zoologist

My racehorse Son Of A Gunner winning its first race. I think it was at Warwick, the price was 16–1 and I've never, before or since, known such joy at a sporting occasion.

It's a ridiculous feeling of elation when your horse wins — because you've done nothing yourself. Why does it give such pleasure? Maybe it's the cost of running the damn thing! Seriously, in this case it was more the vindication of my belief in the animal.

POLLY MURRAY
First Scottish Woman to the summit of Everest

It was 10.30 am on May 16th, 2000, and ahead of me lay huge wave-like cornices of snow.

 I was close to reaching the highest point in the world. I knew within one hour that I would be standing on that point and it felt good.

JIMMY NAIRN
Former head technician, Waid Academy

One of the most memorable moments of my football career was while playing for Glenrothes Juniors in 1967/68. We drew 1–1 with Shotts Bon Accord at Dovecote Park in the quarter finals of the Scottish Junior Cup. The replay was the following Saturday at Hannah Park, Shotts and we went as underdogs.

The rain poured down for most of the game and with seven minutes to go we were one goal down. However, we scored two late goals to get through to the semi-finals. Could it be that Shotts were bad losers? We had no hot water to shower with!

We won the semi 4–0 against Larkhall Thistle but unfortunately lost to Johnstonburgh in the Hampden Final.

STEVE NICOL
Former Ayr United, Liverpool and Scotland foot-baller

The favourite memory of my playing days would be the 1981 victory over England at Wembley. John Robertson scored the goal from the spot but what I remember most is looking at the crowd and seeing tartan scarves and Scottish supporters everywhere. This was the year when the FA tried to ban our supporters, but clearly didn't succeed!

My best memory outwith my playing career was as a boy, watching Lachie Stewart and Ian Stewart come first and second for Scotland at the Commonwealth Games held in Edinburgh in 1970.

Lachie Stewart, 10,000-metre winner Commonwealth games 1970
© SMG Newspapers Ltd

SIR JOHN ORR
Chairman, Kilmarnock Football Club

My most memorable sporting occasion has to be the final game of the league championship on April the 24th 1965 at Tynecastle between Hearts and my home team Kilmarnock Football Club who I have supported from childhood. Killie had to win by two clear goals to win the title otherwise Hearts would be the champions.

I was ecstatic when our young winger Tommy McLean

Kilmarnock FC, Scottish League Champions 1965
© Scottish Daily Record

sent over a cross, which was headed home by Davie Sneddon to put us one up. Minutes later Brian McIlroy put us two ahead with a well-played shot, 2–0 the result that we needed. It was far from over, well into injury time, when Hearts' blond striker Alan Gordon fired in a shot which was brilliantly turned round the post by the prince of goalkeepers – Bobby Ferguson. Kilmarnock had won the League Championship for the first time in their history. The cheers that greeted Frank Beattie and the team could be heard back in Ayrshire.

STEVE PATERSON

Manager, Inverness Caledonian Thistle Football Club

As a player, my most memorable occasions were firstly making my 1st team debut for Manchester United against Sunderland in 1976 at the age of 18. A dream

Victory for Inverness Caledonian Thistle

come true for any young lad. The other most memorable time was playing in the Japanese National Cup Final in Tokyo in 1985 and scoring a goal in a 2–0 victory. A medal presented by the Emperor added to this memory.

As a manager, beating Celtic 3–1 at Parkhead in the Scottish Cup in February 2000 was an obvious highlight that will remain with me forever.

© SMG Newspapers Ltd

DEREK RAE
BBC Scotland commentator 1986–1991 and ESPN commentator 1994 to present

One memory stands out more than any other and it would be Aberdeen's incredible victory over Bayern Munich at Pittodrie in the quarter final second leg of the Cup Winner's Cup in 1983. The Dons went on to win the trophy with an all-Scottish team managed by Alex Ferguson but the win over Bayern was especially dramatic. Trailing 2–1, Aberdeen looked down and out, only to turn the game on its head within the space of 2 incredible minutes. The crowd had barely calmed down after the equaliser when super sub John Hewitt netted the winner and there was no way they were going to lose it after that. As an Aberdonian teenager at the time, this was something very special.

BOBBY RAESIDE
Former Dundee FC Footballer

My most memorable sporting moment as a player would probably be a League Cup tie against Dundee United at Tannadice Park at the beginning of season 1996–97 (I think!)

I had just signed for Dundee from Raith Rovers in the summer, Dundee were in the first Division then and had just lost players of the calibre of Morton Weighorst, Neil McCann and had sold Neil Duffy, their captain to United, who I had been signed to replace, so you could say we were definite underdogs against United in the Premier League.

It was a typical derby game being played at an incredible pace – end-to-end football – great for the fans but tiring for the players! It was 2–2 after extra-time and we won on penalties (I stayed well away from them!)

But what made it just a little bit special to me was the fact that as a boy I used to go and watch United in the big European nights of the eighties, during which time I trained in their Youth set-up but was never offered a contract. So to go to Tannadice under the floodlights and get one over on them was tremendous! It also helped me establish myself with the Dundee fans at my new club.

IAN RANKIN
Crime writer famous for the *Inspector Rebus* novels

Like a lot of people, I thought I had no interest in curling. Like a lot of people, I sat up into the wee small hours to watch the British women's team capturing gold at the Winter Olympics in 2002, leaping from my chair when Rhona Martin's final stone secured an extraordinary victory, a victory snatched from what had at times seemed the jaws of defeat. It was utterly refreshing, as we are a country which all too often seems to snatch defeat from the jaws of victory.

The fact that a certain Janice Rankin was on the team only added to the sweetness. We're not related, but that hardly matters.

Gold medal for the British Women's curling team   © SMG Newspapers Ltd

JANICE RANKIN
Gold medal winner, British Women's Olympic curling team 2002

My best sporting memory comes from the Olympic Games, Salt Lake City, USA, 2002 with our curling team: me, Fiona MacDonald, Debbie Knox and Rhona Martin.

I felt calm, but excited. Rhona was making her way down the ice towards us, and we were all preparing for the last stone of the final of the Olympic Games. Actually, the importance of the shot didn't go through my mind at all, we were just trying to win a curling game.

I knew what we needed to do – we had to catch a piece of the Swiss stone and roll our stone slightly, in order to lie shot.

So, Rhona sat in the hack, Fiona and I had our stopwatches ready, and Debbie was giving the ice. As soon as Rhona let the stone go I knew the weight was good, and Fiona and I called it as the stone travelled down the ice. Debbie started to call for line – we were getting nearer the house and I looked up to see her screaming – oh God, I thought, we really need to sweep this so it doesn't draw too much. So sweep it we did, and the result was perfect. I remember jumping in the air and then hugging Fiona and Debbie. We shook hands with the opposition, and then celebrated with Rhona as well. Our coaches ran onto the ice to be with us. The noise in the arena was amazing and I looked across to the spectators to see a sea of GB flags and everyone jumping about and cheering for us. It was amazing – we were Olympic Champions. Things from then on were a buzz – we had the flower ceremony at the ice rink, an interview for BBC with Hazel Irvine, a press conference and then it was off to Salt Lake City for the medal ceremony. This was the greatest moment of my curling career.

Walking onto the platform with 30,000 people in front of me was an unbelievable feeling. The Canadians got their bronze medals, the Swiss their silvers, and then we got our golds. I sang my heart out to God Save the Queen and thought I was doing a good job keeping myself together, however at the end of the Anthem my emotions got the better of me and the tears of sheer elation came.

I don't think anything I will ever do again will surpass the amazing feeling I had that night, standing on the gold medal podium at Medals Plaza in downtown Salt Lake City, USA. February 21st 2002 will be a day which will forever be in my memory."

ADAM REID
Partner of New Start (English Language School), Rio de Janeiro, Brazil. Information coordinator/site contact for Brazilian football, ESPN International. Waid Academy former pupil

The evening of the 26th September 1973 will always remain in my memory (actually 29 years ago to the day as I write this). That was when Scotland beat Czechoslovakia 2–1 at Hampden to qualify for the 1974 World Cup.

I watched the game in the living room with my dad and two of my brothers – David and Brian. We watched the game on STV with Arthur Montford at his peak. It was "Disaster for Scotland!" when the Czechs opened the scoring, but Jim Holton tied it up with one of his trademark headers just before half-time.

The second half as I recall was very nerve wracking and when, near the end, Bremner hit the post ("Unbelievable misfortune for Scotland!") I remember thinking that we weren't going to do it. I said something to that effect to which David replied "There's still time," and sure enough up popped sub Joe Jordan to head the winner. ("Magnificent Scotland, Magnificent")

I remember rolling around the carpet ecstatic with joy. Looking back, I always thought that it was a last minute winner, however checking the records Jordan actually scored in the 75th minute. I have no recollection of that final 15 mins or so.

Of my own sporting life I have to go for when I was made captain of the Waid 1st XV in 1978. Of all the games that year, winning the Waid–Morgan Cup for the first time in the school's history was a high point. It happened on the 18th November, 1978 at Waid Park and Waid, as usual against Morgan High, were very much the underdogs. We won 14–4.

The 1st XV of '78/'79 was probably one of Waid's finest ever, and had it not been for a teacher's work-to-rule, would have smashed all records. I can still name the side: McClelland, Tarvet, Stephen, Mawson, Fairley, Mackenzie, Gen, Kell, Pollock, Dickson, Smith, Stephenson, Robb, Reid and Barnes. A great team.

As I recall we only used three subs that season – Barnett, Shedden and Buchanan.

A side most of whom had been taught the basics by Eddie MacGeachy five years earlier and then subsequently brought on and perfected by Urqhuart, Herd and of course Norrie MacArthur. Great memories.

GRAEME ROBERTSON
Dunfermline Athletic Football Club

My best sporting memory was when I played for Dunfermline against Rangers in the Scottish Cup in 1988 at East End Park. Big Jim Leishman took us to St Andrews and we stayed at the Old Course hotel.

He sat us down one night and told us one of his poems. He told us all to believe, that on a Saturday we could beat the mighty Rangers, who were littered with great players, Graeme Souness, Richard Gough, Davie Cooper, Mark Walters, Chris Woods to name a few. Well we did believe and won 2–0 with goals from Mark Smith and John Watson.

JOHN ROBERTSON
Assistant Football Manager, Celtic Football Club

My most memorable sporting occasion as a player was the Scotland vs England match in 1981 when we beat England 1–0 and I scored the penalty.

A triumphant John Robertson in 1981   © Scottish Daily Record

DR JAMES ROBSON
Medical Adviser to the British Lions

1997, second test South Africa vs British and Irish Lions. Natal's stadium in Durban. 1–0 to the Lions. Still the South African press expect/demand a home win.

Unbelievable tension in the dressing room, never mind in the ground. Kick-off is a blur, green shirts everywhere; covered by red!

Guscott in the wrong position at the right time. A drop-kick that travelled in time suspended. A "Last stand", the like of which could have saved the Alamo, and it was series win.

A place in rugby history for a group of people brought together by the code Trust and Honesty.

DAVID ROLLO
Scotland rugby player

I was a travelling reserve for Scotland v Ireland, 1959 at Murrayfield. The next game was England v Scotland at Twickenham.

Tuesday morning, 10th March, 1959, the brown SRU envelope arrived. What would it be?

England v Scotland: "You have been selected to play on Saturday, 21st March, 1959.

"Meet, North British Hotel Edinburgh, Thursday 19th March at 10.30 am. Travel to Heathrow, transfer to Hyde Park Hotel. Friday, train at St Paul's School. Theatre at night." I did not sleep well that night.

On Saturday morning, I left for Twickenham after breakfast. We stopped for lunch at Richmond. After lunch a police escort arrived to take us the rest of the way to Twickenham for the game at 3 pm.

Fifteen minutes into the game I had to go off the field with a broken nose. There were no reserves then. Luckily they were able to stuff huge amounts of cotton wool up my nose and I was able to go back on the field and finish the game: three-all.

A great night followed at the Mayfair Hotel. What a weekend!

RONALDO
[RONALDO LUIZ NAZARIO DE LIMA]

Inter Milan and Brazil football teams. World Cup winner in 1994 and in 2002, runner up in 1998. World Player of the Year in 1996 and 1997

My first official appearance for Inter Milan after being out for 17 months with a knee injury was very important to me. It was on the 20th of September 2001 against Brasov in the UEFA Cup. It was in Milan and I came on as a sub and played the last 30 mins. It was my first appearance since April 12, 2000, and many people had written me off, saying I would never be the same again.

Then there was the World Cup in Korea and Japan. After the sadness of losing the final in 1998 in France and then the knee injuries which kept me from playing very many games for more than two years prior to the Cup, well ... many people did not think I would be good enough or fit enough to play in Korea and Japan. But I had faith, my physio, Nilton Petrone, had faith and thankfully so did the coach Luiz Felipe Scolari. Because of the doubts, every game I played was a personal victory but it was the whole squad that won the Cup. To win the greatest competition unbeaten was enough. To be the top scorer and score two goals in the final against Germany was like something out of Holly wood.

Another fantastic moment was the winning of the World Cup in the United States in 1994. Although I did not play in any of the games, just to be part of the group was fantastic. The unity in the group that had players like Romario, Bebeto and Dunga was great.

Brazil had waited 24 years for their fourth cup. I was just 17 years old and I was running round the field in Los Angeles with the World Cup in my hands.

JOHN ROWBOTHAM
Premier League Football Referee

As a fresh-faced youngster in his first season as a junior referee, the prospect of a St Andrews v Newburgh game was, on paper, quite straightforward. But I had not bargained for a gentleman named Norrie McArthur in the technical area (the dugout in old money) who that morning had obviously got out of bed on the wrong side.

Here was a manager who on the day seemed to think that every decision given against his team by me was wrong, i.e., more than he normally thought.

As the match wore on, the normally placid Norrie McArthur became more animated towards me, until I decided that enough was enough. So when play stopped, I wandered over and invited Mr McArthur to join me on the touchline for a chat! Mistake no 1. He declined and instead invited me to join him in the dugout!

I went over and leaned in, top half in, bottom half out. Mistake no 2. On trying to calm him down, he uttered the well-know football phrase "Hurry up and get on with the game". Now what do I do? (thinks quickly – get out of here). A few more hasty words of warning and then I left the dugout, with Norrie mumbling a few more words of disagreement.

You taught me a lesson that day Norrie, never go near a manager in a bad mood!

ALEX SALMOND
SNP Westminster Group Leader

Tennents Scottish Cup Final, 16 May 1998, before a crowd of nearly 49,000 at Celtic Park, Heart of Midlothian Football Club beat Glasgow Rangers 2–1.

I had my first taste of success with Hearts in their League Cup final win in 1962, when Norrie Davidson scored the only goal of the match to beat Kilmarnock. I went to the game with my dad, who forecast more title wins in the future.

Little did I think that we'd have to wait another 36 years to see the fulfilment of his prophecy!

Next time round, I took my dad to the game – the first cup final we'd attended together since the glory days of 1962.

The omens were right for a Hearts win – they had a confidence about them that came from the success they'd enjoyed throughout the year, and Rangers – it had been proved – were no longer invincible. Moreover, Jim Jeffries – the man I'd watched as a player in the 1970's – had built a solid side.

Colin Cameron got us off to a dream start, with a penalty fired high into Goram's net in under two minutes. And Stephane Adam sealed it ten minutes into the second half, with an angled shot that bounced under Goram.

McCoist's late goal made for a scary last few minutes, as Rangers came back with a vengeance. I'll never forget

Hearts v Rangers 1998, John Robertson and goal hero Colin Cameron   © Eric McCowat/Scottish Daily Record

the Celtic director sitting next to me who vowed that he'd remain neutral throughout. As soon as it looked like Rangers might equalise, he was on his feet rooting for Hearts, as if he'd been a Jambo all his life! At full time, this erstwhile "neutral" fan presented me with a bottle of Celtic champagne as a memento of the day. But the Hearts win was sweeter than any champagne, and made for a day that I'll never forget.

LUIZ FELIPE SCOLARI

Nickname in English-speaking countries, 'Big Phil', nickname in Brazil, Felipão, coach of 2002 World Cup winning team Brazil

MY first sporting memories were of Brazilian tennis player Maria Esther Bueno winning at Wimbledon back in the 1960's.

I can remember I saw the odd Maria Esther Bueno game but it was so distant, so far away.

Other memories include Brazil's volleyball (men's) Gold medal at the Barcelona Olympics, the basketball team beating the United States at the 1987 Panam games to win the gold medal and Gustavo Kuerten winning the French Open for the first time.

Our gold medal in Barcelona with the volleyball team, our basketball gold medal with Oscar (Schmidt) in Indianapolis, the 1958 World Cup with Pele, (even though there was no television) – these and the image of Guga (Kuerten), his humility, his simple way of being – winning the title and giving the ball that big hit into the sky."

I also enjoy playing tennis and volleyball with my friends in my spare time.

Volleyball's good – nobody knows how to play and we all enjoy ourselves. If I play football, I just end up getting into a fight.

My personal favourite memory in which I was involved – before the World Cup final in 2002 which tops the lot – was the Libertores Cup I won with Palmeiras. Moreso than the once I won with Gremio in 1995 because Gremio had already won the competition. Palmeiras beat Deportivio Cali on penalties. The celebration was incredible. One TV shot I remember was of a boy called Enzo, when Palmeiras scored the winner. One minute he was down in the dumps and the next he was crying with happiness. It was a wonderful picture, it was something you don't forget.

JOCKY SCOTT

Former player with Dundee and Aberdeen and former manager of Dundee, Notts County and Raith Rovers

I have many memorable moments to recall, but one that stands out was in season 1976–77, the League Cup semi-final at Hampden Park, Aberdeen v Rangers.

The score was 5–1 in Aberdeen's favour and I scored a hat-trick. Two goals early in the first half and the third late in the game with goals from Drew Jarvie and Joe Harper sandwiched between.

We went on to beat Celtic 2–1 in the final.

Jocky Scott   © Scottish Daily Record

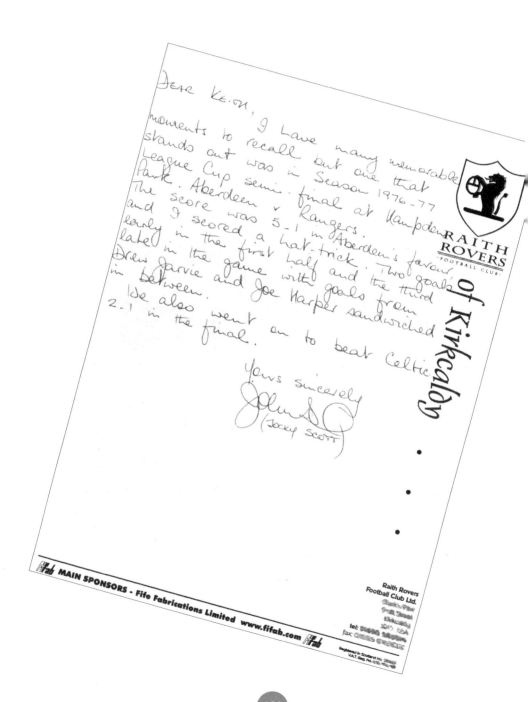

Dear Keith, I have many memorable moments to recall but one that stands out was in Season 1976-77 League Cup semi-final at Hampden Park. Aberdeen v Rangers. The score was 5-1 in Aberdeen's favour and I scored a hat-trick. Two goals early in the first half and the third late in the game with goals from Drew Jarvie and Joe Harper sandwiched in between. We also went on to beat Celtic 2-1 in the final.

Yours sincerely
John S (Jocky Scott)

RAITH ROVERS
FOOTBALL CLUB

of Kirkcaldy

TOMMY SHERIDAN
MSP for Glasgow, Scottish Socialist Party

My most memorable sporting occasion was probably the promotion from second division of the Abercorn Central Junior League four sessions ago. I was playing with East Kilbride Thistle and we had been written off several months previously as far as promotion place was concerned.

However, we were on a tremendous run in the last twelve matches of the season however, which gave us an

Scottish Socialist firebrand Tommy Sheridan, centre, shows he's also a formidable character on the football field
© Scottish Daily Record

opportunity in the final game to either beat or draw with Port Glasgow at home in order to secure promotion. If, however, we were beaten, then we would not have secured promotion. Port Glasgow had been the high fly- ers throughout the season but now found themselves requiring at least one point to also secure promotion.

The game was very well attended at East Kilbride Thistle's park in East Kilbride with approaching 1,000 spectators on a very sunny day. It was a hard game and we took the lead early in the second half, only to lose a goal within 15 or 20 minutes. However, we secured a win with the second goal and thereby guaranteed ourselves promotion in second place, prevented Port Glasgow securing promotion and allowing another team, St Anthony's from Govan to join us in the first division. The celebrations were tremendous and this probably counts as my most memorable sporting occasion.

ALEXANDER SMITH
Manager of Ross County Football Club

The most memorable event which springs to my mind has to be winning the second division league in 1977 with Stirling Albion, as this was my first major achievement as a manager. It was a feeling of great jubilation and achievement after much hard work.

EBBE SKOVDAHL
Former manager Brondby, Benfica and Aberdeen

My favourite sporting memory was when I was manager of Brondby and we beat Liverpool 1–0 at Anfield in the UEFA Cup. This happened back in 1995 and it was an unforgettable experience.

The best moment of my sporting career was winning the first championship with Brondby in 1988.

I know that both memories relate to personal experiences but I could not separate the two!

Ebbe Skovdahl   © Scottish Daily Record

March 19, 2002

Keith McCartney
Waid Academy

Dear Keith,

Ebbe Skovdahl has asked me to reply to your kind letter asking him for his favourite sporting memory.

Ebbe was a Liverpool fan as a youngster, so his favourite memory is taking Brondby, then quite an unfashionable Danish club, to Anfield in 1995 and winning 1-0 courtesy of a late Dan Eggen goal. This result was good enough to see Brondby into the third round of the UEFA Cup after the sides had drawn 0-0 in Copenhagen.

Ebbe remembers the game as being a very close encounter with his side soaking up a lot of pressure and proving very dangerous on the break.

Although he's now firmly an Aberdeen fan, Ebbe says this, to date, is his favourite memory match although he's very hopeful this can be surpassed by the Dons doing something special in Europe – hopefully next season!

On a personal note, being Elgin born myself, I remember Norrie McArthur playing at Borough Briggs for the Black and Whites and consequently join Ebbe and everyone here at Pittodrie in wishing you every success with the book.

Best regards

Andrew Shinie
Press Officer

Aberdeen Football Club plc
PITTODRIE STADIUM, ABERDEEN AB24 5QH

Reception · Facsimile · Call Centre
www.afc.co.uk · Club Shop · e mail feedback@afc.co.uk · Club Call · AFC Events

GRAEME SOUNESS

Former Rangers, Liverpool and Tottenham midfielder, capped 54 times for Scotland. Manager of Blackburn Rovers Football Club

My most memorable sporting occasion was in 1984 winning the European Cup as Captain of Liverpool in Rome. We were unfancied, as the game was in their Stadium. The score was 1–1.

It came to a penalty shootout, which we won and I scored one of the penalties. This was my last kick of the ball for Liverpool – after that I was transferred to Sampdoria in Italy.

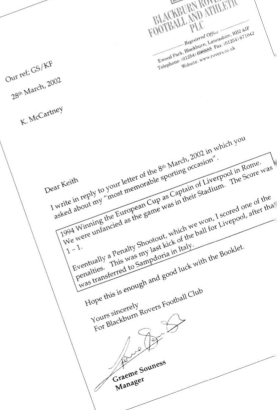

BLACKBURN ROVERS
FOOTBALL AND ATHLETIC
PLC

Registered Office
Ewood Park, Blackburn, Lancashire. BB2 4JF
Telephone: (01254) 698888 Fax: (01254) 671042
Website: www.rovers.co.uk

Our ref; GS/KF

28th March, 2002

K. McCartney

Dear Keith

I write in reply to your letter of the 8th March, 2002 in which you asked about my "most memorable sporting occasion".

1994 Winning the European Cup as Captain of Liverpool in Rome. We were unfancied as the game was in their Stadium. The Score was 1 – 1.

Eventually a Penalty Shootout, which we won, I scored one of the penalties. This was my last kick of the ball for Liverpool, after that was transferred to Sampdoria in Italy.

Hope this is enough and good luck with the Booklet.

Yours sincerely
For Blackburn Rovers Football Club

Graeme Souness
Manager

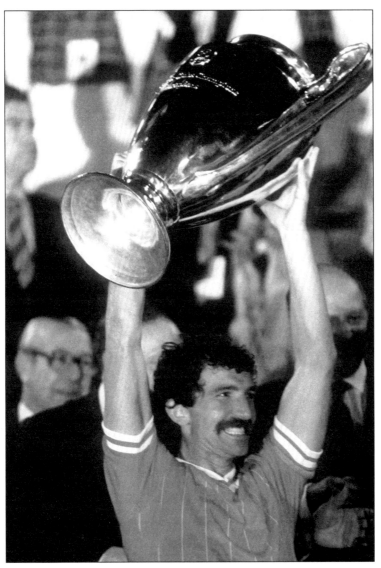

Graeme Souness, proudly holding aloft the European Cup for Liverpool, 1984   © Scottish Daily Record

BILLY STARK
Manager of St Johnstone Football Club

My favourite moment in my career was beating Dundee United at Hampden Park in the 1988 Scottish Cup Final to secure the League and Cup double for Celtic in their Centenary year. The dramatic fashion in which we won the game (equalising with 5 minutes to go then scoring the winner in the last minute) heightened the euphoric feeling in such an historic year for the club.

Celtic v Dundee, Scottish Cup Final, 1988   © SMG Newspapers Ltd

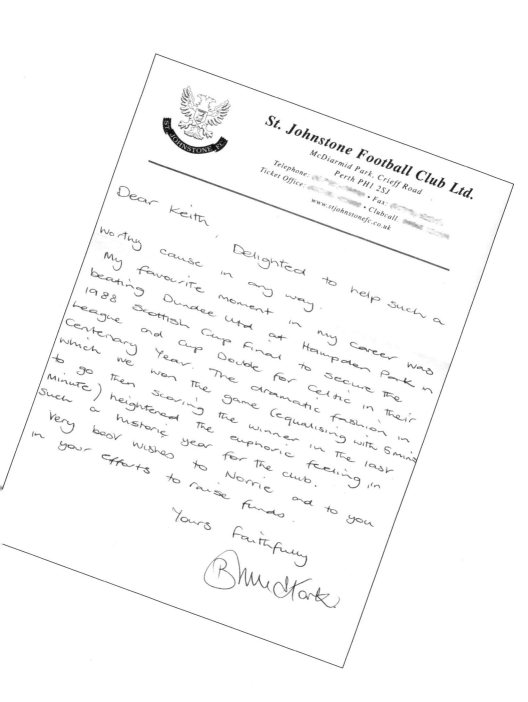

St. Johnstone Football Club Ltd.

McDiarmid Park, Crieff Road
Perth PH1 2SJ

Telephone:
Ticket Office:
• Fax:
• Clubcall:
www.stjohnstonefc.co.uk

Dear Keith,

Delighted to help such a worthy cause in any way.

My favourite moment in my career was beating Dundee Utd at Hampden Park in 1988 Scottish Cup Final to secure the League and Cup Double for Celtic in their Centenary Year. The dramatic fashion in which we won the game (equalising with 5 mins to go then scoring the winner in the last minute) heightened the euphoric feeling in such a historic year for the club.

Very best wishes to Norrie and to you in your efforts to raise funds.

Yours faithfully

Billy McStay

The Scottish Parliament

The Rt Hon Sir David Steel KBE MSP
The Presiding Officer

EDINBURGH
EH99 1SP

Mr Keith McCartney
The Waid Academy

Dear Mr. McCartney,

Thank you very much for your letter of 7th March and I would be delighted to contribute to your booklet to raise funds for Norrie McArthur who suffers from Motor Neurone Disease.

I have no memorable sporting occasions from school. I was equally hopeless at compulsory cricket, hockey and rugby and treasure a school report which says I "play a fair game for the remainders".

I once took part in a televised football match in Edinburgh, celebrities versus professionals. It was a disaster because while we thought it was for entertainment, they took it seriously. I was black and blue in several places for weeks afterwards!

David Steel

SIR DAVID STEEL KBE, MSP
Presiding Officer of the Scottish Parliament, MSP for the Lothians

I have no memorable sporting occasions from school. I was equally hopeless at compulsory cricket, hockey and rugby and treasure a school report which says I "play a fair game for the remainders".

I once took part in a televised football match in Edinburgh, celebrities versus professionals. It was a disaster because while we thought it was for entertainment, they took it seriously. I was black and blue in several places for weeks afterwards!

SIR JACKIE STEWART
Racing driver

I suppose I will always remember winning my first World Championship in Formula One and no doubt I will always remember my third World Championship victory as I knew it was going to be my last.

I have always said that the disappointment of losing my position in the two-man British Olympic trap shooting team for the 1960 Olympic Games in Rome was something that I would never forget. I was having a very successful year of shooting but had one off-day in the final elimination shoot. I was firmly in second place and therefore in the team with one event to go when I lost my timing in one of the four disciplines of 25 targets that day. I was 21 and although I was shooting for the four-man British team I would dearly have liked to have carried the Olympic symbol on my shooting jacket.

It is funny how losing the Indianapolis 500 shortly before the end had no real impact on me or losing the Belgium Grand Prix on the last lap, or even losing a world championship in Formula One did not mean as much.

In life you have to take the highs with the lows and you surely learn a lot from both.

Sir JACKIE STEWART, O.B.E.

Telephone
Facsimile

Mairi Hughes
Office Administrator
Scottish Motor Neurone Disease Association

14 August 2002

Dear Mairi

Here are some of my thoughts of my sporting memories for inclusion in the Scottish Motor Neurone Disease Association booklet.

I suppose winning my first world championship in Formula One I will always remember and no doubt I will always remember my third world championship victory as I knew it was going to be my last. I have always said that the disappointment of losing my position in the two man British Olympic trap shooting team for the 1960 Olympic Games in Rome was something that I would never forget. I was having a very successful year of shooting but had one off day in the final elimination shoot. I was firmly in second place and therefore in the team with one event to go when I lost my timing in one of the four disciplines of 25 targets that day. I was 21 and although I was shooting for the 4 man British team I would dearly have liked to have carried the Olympic symbol on my shooting jacket. It is funny how losing the Indianapolis 500 shortly before the end had no real impact on me or losing the Belgium Grand Prix on the last lap, or even losing a world championship in Formula One did not mean as much. In life you have to take the highs with the lows and you surely learn a lot from both.

Yours sincerely

[signature]

JACK STRAW
Foreign Secretary

My most memorable sporting occasion was on 14th May 1995 at Annfield, where Blackburn Rovers lost their match against Liverpool but won the Premiership.

It was the final day of the season, and we needed to win to guarantee that Rovers were champions. But, it was Liverpool who ran out winners, and so we had to endure a nail-biting wait before discovering that our main rivals Manchester United had only managed to draw with West Ham at Upton Park and our result made no difference. We had lost a game, but won the Championship. What a day!

It was a tremendous moment, and one I will never forget.

20th March 2002

Foreign &
Commonwealth
Office

London SW1A 2AH

From The Secretary of State

Dear Mr. McCartney,

Thank you for your letter asking me to describe my most memorable sporting occasion.

I have no hesitation in telling you that it was on 14th May 1995 at Anfield where Blackburn Rovers lost their match against Liverpool but won the Premiership.

It was the final day of the season, and we needed to win to guarantee that Rovers were champions. But, it was Liverpool who ran out winners, and so we had to endure a nail-biting wait before discovering that our main rivals Manchester United had only managed to draw with West Ham at Upton Park and our result made no difference. We had lost a game, but won the Championship. What a day!

It was a tremendous moment, and one I will never forget.

Yours sincerely

JACK STRAW

Mr Keith McCartney
The Waid Academy

GRAHAM TAYLOR
Manager, Aston Villa and former England manager

I have been very fortunate to be involved in many memorable occasions during my career, both as a football player and as a football manager – especially the latter.

One of the most memorable is when I rejoined Watford as their manager when they were a second division club. We won the second division championship and the next season found ourselves in the final play-off game against Bolton Wanderers at Wembley.

We won the game 2–0, and after the match, as I walked off the Wembley pitch, I turned round and witnessed over 36,000 Watford supporters waving their very bright colours of yellow, red and black. This is a picture that will remain with me for the rest of my life.Having said that, I often wonder that as Vicarage Road, which is Watford's stadium, only holds 22,500 people, where did those 14,000 supporters come from.

Manager's Office

ASTON VILLA

Our ref:- GT/DAR

18th March, 2002

Mr. K. McCartney,
The Waid Academy,
Anstruther,
FIFE. KY10 3HD

Dear Mr. McCartney,

Thank you for your letter dated 8th March, 2002.

As you will see, I am enclosing a memorable sporting occasion on a separate piece of paper.

Best wishes.

Yours sincerely,

GRAHAM TAYLOR,
MANAGER.

ASTON VILLA PLC
Villa Park, Birmingham, B6 6HE

Registered in England No. 40...

JIMMY TARBUCK
Comedian

Liverpool reached the final of the FA Cup and played Leeds United at Wembley Stadium. I invited Frankie Vaughan, who I was working with at the time, to come along. We met Bill Shankly and the team in the dressing room, wished them luck and took our seats.

An excellent game followed, and at full time it was 1–1. Frankie wanted to leave at this point, but there was no way I was going to miss extra time.

In the closing minutes, Ian St John scored. Liverpool had won the FA Cup Final for the first time!

A helicopter was on hand to take Frankie and I back to Coventry where we were doing the show. But as there was a very high wind, the helicopter was very small and I valued my life, I refused to get in the thing.

We decided it would be safer to take a taxi from Wembley to Coventry, but it broke down on the M6. We decided to hitch a lift, but didn't have much luck.

I suggested that Frankie perform his famous high kicks at the side of the road to see if this would help.

Sure enough a car stopped for us! Frankie sat beside a very pregnant lady who could not quite believe she was sharing a car with the great Frankie Vaughan!

RIGHT HONOURABLE LORD NORMAN TEBBIT
Member of the House of Lords

When I became Secretary of State for Employment in 1981 I was told that the department played an annual cricket match against the newspaper, radio and television industrial correspondents, and the Secretary of State was expected to captain his side.

Mercifully – for I am an appallingly poor cricketer – the match was rained off in my first year. In 1983, however, it was played and my department lost by something like 170 runs to 150.

There was considerable controversy at that time over some changes in the way in which statistics of unemployment were collected and of some of the seasonal adjustments that were made, so at the end of the match, I announced the scores.

My department 150, the media correspondents 170 – but after seasonal adjustments the scores became my department 170, the media 150, so my department had won.

JIM TELFER
Scottish Rugby Union

In a fairly long career both as a player and coach I obviously had many special occasions. Being the coach of the winning Grand Slam team in 1984 was obviously a highlight, as was being coach to Melrose club side who won their first championships in 1990 season.

However, without any shadow of doubt, the most memorable occasion was the 1997 Lions victory in Durban in the second Test, giving the Lions an unassailable 2–0 lead in the Test series against the Springboks. Having played for the Lions on two losing tours as a player and once as a coach, the result wiped out all the bad memories of former Lions failures.

Against the odds the Lions had won the first test in Cape Town. The victory had been unconvincing as far as the South African public was concerned, who fully expected their team to reverse the results the following week. As it turned out, the game was a cliffhanger with the lead changing on many occasions right up to the last few minutes when a draw seemed the likely result. However, the Lions on that day had other ideas. The team forced its way down into the Springbok 22, and when Gregor Townsend won a ruck just to the left hand side of the posts, the ball came back from Matt Dawson to Gerry Guscott in an unfamiliar roll as stand off with very few options. In a twinkling, he decided what to do and the most unlikely drop goal sailed between the posts to give the Lions the lead with time running out. The final whistle went a few minutes later with the score 18–15 in the Lions favour and a crescendo of noise was unleashed by the thousands of red-shirted Lion supporters celebrating the first Test series victory in South Africa for over 20 years.

My career as a Lion ended on the highest note possible.

Jim Telfer in a celebratory mood   © Scottish Daily Record

FULHAM FOOTBALL CLUB

CRAVEN COTTAGE   STEVENAGE ROAD   LONDON   SW6 6HH

To Norrie
Best Wishes

From Jean Tigana
and all at Fulham
Football Club

ALEX TOTTEN
Former Manager of Falkirk Football Club

I would probably say that my most memorable sporting occasion was taking Falkirk to the cup final at Ibrox in 1997.

The town was buzzing from the moment we drew with Celtic in the semi-final and then went on to beat them in the replay. There was a total feeling of togetherness, whether you were a Falkirk fan or not. The shops in the town were decorated, people had street parties and the build up to the final was immense.

The atmosphere on arriving at Ibrox in the team bus was electric and 22,000 Falkirk fans attended the game that day. It was also amazing for me personally to see so many Kilmarnock fans waving and wishing me good luck even though we were playing them in the final.

The press described the final as the family final, and, even though we lost that day, the streets on our arrival back at Falkirk were lined with mums, dads, children, and each and every one at the club was proud to be a Falkirk fan.

It is a day I will never forget and will always cherish the memories of.

IAN WHITE
Scottish International Kayaker and Expeditionary

My greatest sporting memory remains Dr Mike Jones and his team making the first full descent of the Dudh Kosi river in Nepal in 1976.

To this day, it remains an outstanding achievement upon which all expeditionary travel by kayak should be measured.

ANN WIDDECOMBE

MP for Maidstone and the Weald, former Shadow Home Secretary

I was utterly hopeless at sports at school. I could swim and ride but neither of these sports were part of the curriculum. Instead; I was obliged to play hockey, in spite of not being able to run very fast, and tennis, in which I found the racquet uncomfortably heavy. I much preferred to spend my time reading Virgil and studying Roman history.

However, each year, the staff used to play the 6th form at hockey. We used to dress up in fairly funny clothes and engage in a lively hockey match for the benefit of the whole school. I played for the 6th form in 1966 and wore a striped shirt and the placard "World Cup Widdie". It was quite surprising that, being normally hopeless at hockey, I excelled myself on that occasion whacking the ball away from the games mistress herself, no less, and passing it to another girl who scored a goal. It was the first time I've ever been cheered on the sports field in the whole of my life and I confidently expect that it will be the last.

J P R WILLIAMS

Former Wales rugby full-back, now a consultant in orthopaedic surgery, Princess of Wales Hospital Bridgend

I have chosen the try scored by Phil Bennett at Murrayfield in 1977 as my favourite sporting memory. I have chosen this because it was a great team try.

As always in those days, the Wales–Scotland game was always played at great pace. I collected a kick ahead from Andy Irvine, the Scotland full back, dived on the ball and managed to pass the ball to Steve Fenwick, who passed to Gerald Davies. Our mercurial wing beat a couple of players before passing on to Phil Bennett, who then passed to David Burcher.

An over-head pass from David Burcher found Phil Bennett again and, with a very neat side-step, he beat the last line of defence and ended up scoring under the post. This score from deep in our own half epitomized the Welsh team of that time, ie, turning desperate defence into attack and ending with a match-winning score under the posts.

TERRY WOGAN
TV and radio presenter

My greatest sporting moment was undoubtedly at Gleneagles, on the Kings Course, playing with Fuzzy Zoeller against Lee Trevino and Trevor Brooking, for Pro-Celebrity Golf, on BBC TV.

On the 18th, having driven into a bush, I took a drop for a penalty, then hit my third to the edge of the huge green.

It was a 33-yard putt, and I sunk it, for a birdie, to win the match. I know that it was 33 yards, because Trevino paced it out, while muttering under his breath in Spanish.

Peter Alliss still refers to it as the longest putt ever seen on television.

HELEN YOUNG
BBC Weather person

As far as sporting moments are concerned I can't say I was ever a great sportswoman but I did turn from being the slouch potato (as my university friends used to call me) to running the London Marathon in 1992. For me that is my greatest sporting moment.

When I started training I couldn't even run 500 yards let alone 26 and a bit miles! That was partly due to lack of fitness but also due to the fact that I suffer from asthma. I was determined though, and I started training in the August before the race in April 1993.

I started running from one lamp post to another and walking the next. Before long I could run between at least 10 lamp posts!! At the time I was living in Crowthorne, Berkshire. On one run I remember running up a road I'd never seen before and ended up outside the gates to Broadmoor!! I've never run so fast home in all my life. Eventually I started running further and in the November I entered the Camberley half marathon. I completed it in 2 hours 15 minutes. After that I was determined to finish the marathon.

On the day of the marathon I just remember rubbing Vaseline into all my creases (don't worry everyone does it!!) and then feeling completely ill, wondering what I had let myself in for. In fact I cried in the car on the way to it. I thought I wouldn't be able to do it! However by the time I arrived at start I was really elated. All the competitors were on a high just wanting to get it over and done with. I remember starting the race with another girl called Helen but we were parted at 14 miles! The atmosphere as I was running was incredible. So many people watching and cheering. It really spurred me on.

At 23 miles, just as I was flagging I bumped into a guy who was also struggling. Together we were determined to finish, we encouraged each other and without him I don't think I would have made it.

The sad thing is I can't even remember his name but I shall always be grateful to him for making my dreams of completing the London marathon come true. By running the London Marathon I raised £5000 for the Guillain Barre Syndrome Support Group, far surpassing my expectations.

ZICO [ARTHUR ANTURES COIMBRA]
Brazilian midfielder

My favourite sporting achievement was scoring the two goals for Flamengo in the final of the Copa Libertadores against Cobreloa of Chile in 1981.

It meant Flamengo won the most important club tournament in South America for the first, and up to now, the only time.

It was the third game of the final. We had won the first leg on November 13, 2–1 at the Maracana but lost 1–0 in Santiago the following week. Neither away goals nor penalties were used to decide the outcome so it went to a third game in neutral country.

On November 23, we met the very strong Chileans at the Centenario Stadium, Montevideo Uruguay. It was a very tough game but I scored in the 18th and 79th minutes and we won the Libertadores.

Although we went on to beat Liverpool 3–1 later that year in Japan for the World Club championship, it was that night in Montevideo that was the most important for me.